MOTIVATING
YOUR STUDENTS

MOTIVATING YOUR STUDENTS

Before You Can Teach Them, You Have to Reach Them

HANOCH McCARTY

FRANK SICCONE

ALLYN AND BACON

Boston   London   Toronto   Sydney   Tokyo   Singapore

Editor-in-chief: Karen Hanson
Series editor: Karon Bowers
Series editorial assistant: Jennifer Becker
Marketing manager: Jacqueline Aaron
Composition and prepress buyer: Linda Cox
Manufacturing buyer: Megan Cochran
Cover administrator: Brian Gogolin
Editorial-production service: Karen Mason
Copyeditor: Margaret Pinette
Text designer: Karen Mason
Electronic composition: Karen Mason

ISBN 0-205-32260-3

Printed in the United States of America.
10 9 8 7 6 5 4 3 2 1   05 04 03 02 01 00

Hanoch's Dedication

To all the wonderfully exciting teachers I've had, the ones who saw it as their mission to help make every lesson worthwhile, the ones who were willing to go that one extra step beyond the mere curriculum, those who had the courage to ignore convention, the ones who still had that fire inside. Among them I count: Sidney B. Simon, Carl Auria, Esther Keck Sheldon, Matthew Weinstein, Martin Rutte, Jack Canfield, and my coauthor, Frank Siccone.

Frank's Dedication

This book is dedicated to my maternal grandparents, Louis and Eva Silva. Soon after I was born, when my mother, brother, and I needed a place to stay, my mother's parents took us in. There we all lived until I graduated high school. Since it was the only home I knew, I'm afraid I took my grandparents' generosity for granted.

Now that I am old enough to be a grandfather myself, I can appreciate the sacrifices they made in helping to raise us. When my grandparents should have been enjoying retirement, they were coping with two energetic little boys and their bouts of sibling rivalry all the way through their years of adolescent attitude and angst—not to mention rock music and blue lights in the basement.

I never really said, "Thanks, Vavo and Vavou, for everything."

Contents

Acknowledgments

HANOCH'S ACKNOWLEDGMENTS

I'd like to acknowledge the help I've received as a teacher over the years from Sidney B. Simon, who was the first real mentor in my professional life and who, by raising the bar constantly, encouraged me to take leaps and risks in order to discover for myself that I had fewer limits than I imagined. I cannot ever thank him enough for all he did to help me develop a style of teaching that proved successful in some very difficult environments.

I also must acknowledge one of my most consistent models of great teaching, my wife, Meladee D. McCarty, who helps me learn more and more about the bond of caring that must exist between teacher and student in order for that relationship to realize its full potential.

FRANK'S ACKNOWLEDGMENTS

First, I want to thank my coauthor and friend, Hanoch, for inviting me to work with him on this project. Every time we do something together, I am impressed by his wisdom, tickled by his sense of humor, and touched by his kindness.

Thanks also to my associate, Robert Wright. This is the fifth book for which he has prepared the manuscript. Once again, he has done a brilliant job.

On a more personal note, I wish to acknowledge Esther Wright for her support at crucial moments this year. To Pat Roback and Ricky Capsuto, the highlight of my professional life the last twelve months was coaching the two of you to rediscover your love for each other. And finally thanks are due my partner, Chris Jehle, for always bringing out the best in me.

About the Authors

Hanoch McCarty is an educational psychologist and author of a number of texts such as *Growing Pains in the Classroom: A Guide to Teachers of Adolescents,* as well as popular books such as *A 4th Course of Chicken Soup for the Soul, Chicken Soup for the Grandparent's Soul,* and *Acts of Kindness.* He is a parent of four and a grandparent, too. He taught English and History on the high school level in the inner city as well as suburban schools. He was Associate Professor of Education at Cleveland State University and had previously taught at the University of Hartford and Southern Illinois University at Edwardsville. He is now a private consultant working with school systems across the United States and Canada on issues relating to student and teacher motivation, the enlivenment of instruction, parental and family involvement, as well as the development of self-esteem and its impact on the learning process. He can be reached at hanoch@bestspeaker.com; by mail at PO Box 66, Galt, CA 95632; or by phone at (209) 745-2212.

Frank Siccone is the President of Siccone Institute, which offers programs in personal and professional growth, as well as organizational development training to nonprofit and corporate clients.

With a doctorate in education, Frank has conducted workshops for school administrators, teachers, parents, and students for over 20 years. He has taught at a number of colleges and universities, and is the author of *101 Ways to Develop Student Self-Esteem and Responsibility* (with Jack Canfield); *Educating the Heart: Lessons in Respect and Responsibility* (with Lilia Lopez); and *The Power to Lead: A Guidebook for School Administrators on Facilitating Change.* He has used his knowledge of human motivation to help individuals achieve their career goals, couples to rekindle their love and passion for one another, and businesses to quadruple in size. Now, with this book, Frank collaborates with Hanoch to teach you new ways to motivate your students. You can contact him at fsiccone@aol.com; by phone at (415) 922-2244; or by mail at Siccone Institute, 1201 Greenwich Street, #500, San Francisco, CA 94109.

# **INTRODUCTION**

Start where people are before you
take them where you want them to be.

Anonymous

THE CHALLENGE OF MOTIVATING STUDENTS

You are being invited to become a more motivational teacher.
The thought is oddly troubling. "Who am I to motivate anyone else?" you ponder. Can anyone be motivated by anyone
else? Self-doubt assails you. Sound familiar? It's probably why
you're reading this book.

You wonder as you are planning your lessons, "How can I
motivate this group of students? What can I say or do that
will materially affect their motivations? And just what do I
want them to be motivated to do?"

After all these years of teaching and speaking in front of
audiences from coast to coast, we have come to believe that *it
is nearly impossible to motivate someone else.* Let's pretend that
in front of you is a classroom of students with no motivation
of their own. They all suffer from apathy, boredom, or whatever malaise you can imagine, which either removed their
own natural motivation or prevented them from developing
any. There they sit, immobile, impassive, uncaring. And you
are to motivate them!

Daunting task, isn't it? How can you get your motivation across to them and implanted in them so they will then be motivated? If it sounds impossible, that's because it probably *is* impossible. We don't mean that the task of delivering a motivational lesson is impossible, we just believe that one cannot "give" motivation to someone else *unless one can tap into the motivations already present in that person!* If you could truly assemble a room of totally unmotivated students, you'd find it impossible to motivate them, because you cannot connect with the motivations that aren't already there.

If, on the other hand, you find yourself in front of an actively hostile class, as difficult as it might be to motivate them positively, you at least have a reasonable chance, because they are already powerfully motivated—with their anger, upset, hostility, or whatever set of concerns or problems have left them feeling the way they do. As the teacher entering such a room, if you've done your homework—as we'll explain elsewhere in this book—you can connect with those motivations and possibly turn them around toward positive dimensions.

So the act of motivating students, singly or in groups, demands that you understand and attempt to connect with their feelings, concerns, values, experiences, and unmet needs.

ALL HUMANS ARE MOTIVATED

All humans are motivated by their unmet needs or unfulfilled wants. If you are perfectly content, you will stay where you are, doing what you are doing. It is only when you discover in yourself a need that you rise, look around, and seek the desired object. Sitting in front of your television, you are absorbed in the program. Gradually you become aware of hunger, or thirst, or pressure in your bladder. When one of these needs becomes strong enough to overwhelm your interest in the program, you find yourself going to the refrigerator or to the bathroom. That's called *motivation*.

In order to understand motivation, let us create a scenario: You are at work. You love your job. You've been teaching for only a few years and find yourself increasing in skill and achievement. There's a fascination to every challenge in the job. You are already fully motivated, aren't you? You don't need to attend a motivational talk. In fact, it might be an annoying distraction to take you away from your work today to bring you to a motivating speaker.

Now, let's fast forward in a time machine to five years later. You've been doing this job a long time. There doesn't seem to be any surprises any more. There's been a salary freeze in your school district. The lack of available funding has prevented you from acquiring supplementary materials you know could make a big difference in your teaching. You feel frustrated.

All the teachers in your district are asked to attend a conference. The conference begins with a motivational keynote address. Are you a candidate for motivation? The answer could be a resounding, *YES!* if the speaker is aware of the issues and has good, positive, and reliable information to share. You are ready for motivation because, in this scenario, you may have the following motivations: *boredom* with a job done too long and too predictably—the challenge and fun have faded; *anger,* because you've not been given raises that you feel you deserve; *frustration,* because you have a picture of how to improve your work but lack of funding has blocked you; *fear,* because of possible personnel cuts. All of these feelings are motivations. Equally, you are a candidate for motivation because you have the desire for achievement, a need to reach excellence, a love for the challenge of teaching. You're ready to be motivated because your job, no matter how difficult things have been lately, still represents to you the field you love most and the one you studied for years to master. You remember the good times and are motivated to try to bring the school community back to those times. You may be ready for motivation because you are an upbeat person, one who is always ready to tackle seemingly insurmountable tasks and conquer them. You see, there are many motivations and many reasons that people become motivated.

YOU MUST UNDERSTAND
YOUR STUDENTS' MOTIVATIONS

A teacher, to be successful, has to understand student motivations, be aware of them, and speak to them directly to make learning relevant.

Alex is every teacher's dream. She comes to school prepared to learn. Self-motivated, she needs little direction or encouragement. Her work is always well thought-out, complete, and turned in on time. Alex is motivated by a sense of personal pride in a job well-done. Matthew, on the other hand, brings with him a history of less-than-stellar academic achievement. He has lost his self-confidence and no longer believes he is capable of succeeding. His choice is to accept being a failure or reject school as a measure of self-worth. Being tough, a rebel who doesn't care what teachers say, gives him a certain amount of prestige among his peers. Matthew is motivated by fear and the need to look good.

In every class are students with many different motivations. It is important to realize that not everyone is "on the same page" at the same time motivationally. Some will be "the good students," motivated by their desire to be attentive and please the teacher. Others may be new students who are still disoriented, somewhat confused, anxious about being seen as competent, unsure as to whether they will fit in to the group or if they will succeed. Some students with a long history of failure in school may have dropped out mentally if not physically a long time ago. Others may want to be seen as blasé: "This is boring." We could go on and on: The range of possible motivations and combinations of motivations that may exist in members of a group is nearly infinite. The important fact to remember is: Everyone is motivated by something—unless he or she is in a coma! If you can determine what the major motivations are in this class, you can become a motivational teacher.

MOTIVATION IS NOT A PAINT JOB

The successful motivational teacher doesn't motivate students in the sense of giving them something they didn't have, painting the motivation on their surface. Instead, he or she reaches the students, finds their major motivations or those most appropriate to his or her own educational objectives, and taps into them, using those motivations as the core components of the lesson.

If you are fabulously wealthy and are offered a chance to save $2.00 by bringing in a coupon to the store, it's unlikely you will have been motivated to become a customer. Even with a nice coupon, beautifully printed, you haven't been motivated because your money needs—at least at that level—are fully satisfied. Someone else cannot *give you* a motivation. Picture the moment when you've just eaten and are satisfied; you've pushed away from the table and announced, "I am stuffed." At that moment offering you another steak, perfectly cooked, would be a waste of time, for your food needs are completely satisfied. To motivate you, someone would have to find what wants or needs you still have not fulfilled.

NO ONE MOTIVATES EVERYONE ALL THE TIME

So it is possible to be a motivator. You can make a difference with many, if not all, of the students in your class. There will be some whom you do not and cannot reach—at least not today. The paradox is to teach with the clear intention of inspiring each and every student to discover his or her love of learning and then to accept that some were moved and others were not. Then return to school tomorrow prepared for this to be the day when the awakening happens.

Hanoch had the great privilege some years ago to share the platform at a national conference with the late world-renowned psychologist and author, Carl Rogers. Hanoch confesses that he was so awestruck by this man, whose writings had been a central part of his own training, that his contributions to the discussion were very limited indeed. At one point in the evening Dr. Rogers was asked if his fame had affected his ability to do his work with people. He indicated that it was a continuing problem to have to deal with people putting him on a pedestal and elevating even his most mundane remark into a kind of revealed truth. Nevertheless, he said, it was also seductive to be treated that way, and he constantly struggled to restore himself, in people's eyes, to a common, equal, human perspective without buying in to the level of expertise and magical qualities with which they would try to invest him.

In this context, Dr. Rogers told a story. He said that he had been teaching at a well-known conference and training center on the West Coast in a beautiful room with a whole wall of picture windows facing the ocean. There were over a hundred therapists, psychologists, and other professionals there attending his workshop for the week. He sat on a chair, but most participants sat on the carpeting at his feet. As he was speaking about some psychological insight or other, the room was rapt with attention. Suddenly, one of the participants called out, "Look! A rainbow!" Just like children, the whole group leaped to their feet and ran to the windows to enjoy the sight, leaving Dr. Rogers sitting alone facing the empty spots where his audience had just been. He confessed that he was put out by this and then realized that he was not as free of playing guru as he had thought. He, too, got up and went to see the rainbow. While standing at the window, listening to the oohs and ahhs uttered by many, the man standing nearest to him muttered under his breath, "Awww, this is nothing! This isn't half as nice as the rainbow I saw last month in Hawaii!"

Dr. Rogers smiled as he told this story. "You see," he explained, "for this man, even God Himself deserves a 'C-minus' in rainbow making! There are people out there who cannot be pleased by anyone or anything!"

It is not a reasonable expectation to think you'll ever get to 100 percent of your students. Keep in mind that the business of motivation involves a partnership between you, the teacher or motivator, and the students, each of whom brings his or her own motivations, strong or weak, positive or negative, to the classroom. The moment that you have the opportunity to become a motivational teacher is when you involve yourself in a relationship with your students. As you will see, they want motivation, and you want to be motivating. The trick is going to be whether or not you learn to connect yourself, your words, and your ideas to their need, their background and experiences, their ways of seeing the world. Make that connection, and you will be well on your way to being an excellent motivational teacher.

All teachers use words, gestures, movement, stories, ideas, facts, and techniques to reach their students. You will mold all these elements into a lesson and deliver it, and, if you

speak to the heart of each member of the class, to the heart
and not just to the mind, you will have reached your goal.
You cannot convince your students, by force of reason, by
weight of facts and figures, to become motivated in some
direction. Ideas and facts alone do not motivate well.

Some years ago a study was conducted on people's values.
The researchers, in order to discover what people valued the
most, asked large groups to list what they thought they
would save if they arrived at their homes only to discover
that their homes were on fire. Group after group was asked to
list the first ten items they'd try to rescue. The lists made
enormous sense. People saved their families, their valuables,
and their irreplaceable keepsakes. Some time later, another
researcher, interested in panic behavior, looked at what people actually *did* save when confronted with a house fire. The
lists were considerably less sensible. Several examples are
worth noting: A woman saved a picture of her cat and left
the cat; a man saved a receipt for $10,000 and left the
money; another saved a written description of his valuable
antique violin and left the instrument. When people are calm
and rational their behavior is much different from those
moments when they are emotional and feeling. Similarly, we
are taught to believe that we are motivated by reason, yet
many studies have shown that people's rationales for their
behavior may sound logical but are often created *ex post facto*
to explain otherwise irrational choices. In short, we behave
more out of our hearts than from cold logic. If you would
motivate others, you must become attuned to what touches
the heart.

Hanoch was a high school teacher working at an inner-
city high school in an economically depressed area of New
York City. A big old, shabby building, crammed with many
more students than it was designed for, it was beset with gang
violence and suffered from an often dispirited faculty. He had

taught there only about a year when he came down with pneumonia and had to stay home for two weeks. When he returned, he entered the office to pick up his mail. As he went through the mail in his box, he felt an arm around his shoulders. It was his principal, Paul Balser. He did not know him well. There were over 185 teachers in the building and perhaps 3500 students. Hanoch thought the principal didn't know him at all. He was surprised at his familiarity. The principal said, "We missed you. Glad you're back." "You missed me?" Hanoch replied incredulously, "What do you mean by that? You had a substitute." Mr. Balser smiled, "Oh, we had someone who covered your classes, but we couldn't find anyone who could fill your shoes!" Hanoch didn't even know that Mr. Balser knew anything about him, but there he was telling him that he had something of value to share with kids in his building, that he was *irreplaceable*. After that, Hanoch would have done almost anything for that man. Talk about motivation! Mr. Balser spoke to the heart. All of us crave being valued, making a significant contribution. When Hanoch realized that his attempts to make his English class interesting and enjoyable to his students were recognized by his principal, it lead him to a whole new level of activity, creativity, and extra energy.

Speak to the heart. Find what is at the core of your students' concerns. Keep your eyes and ears tuned to finding out those central, most important feelings, concerns, issues, or values, and speak to them directly. That is the key, the foundation, the secret to the art of motivational teaching.

WHAT MOTIVATES PEOPLE?

A dog wags its tail with its heart.

Martin Buxbaum

If you plan on being a motivational teacher, you would do well to become more aware of what motivates the students you are trying to influence. People have many motivations, some stronger than others. In fact, there is a *hierarchy* of motivations. For example, you might want to improve your ability to speak French and yet, no matter how much you want that, if you are starving, your motivation to eat will be much stronger and more immediately acted upon than your desire for foreign language lessons. Your desire to save your own life is strong but may be superseded by your desire to save your child.

Motivations come in varieties: There are positive and negative motivations; social, physical, emotional, spiritual, and intellectual motivations. There are greed, fear, lust, love, altruism, and the desire for safety. If your students perceive that one or more of these areas is deficient or unfulfilled, and you provide in your teaching some road toward fulfillment of that need, you will have motivated them, and they will not soon forget you and your message. Your lesson does not have to fulfill the need or solve the problem—it simply has to offer a view of how to solve the problem or a route toward the fulfillment of that need, or it has to convince those listening that they have the power to satisfy that need at some time in the future with a reasonable expenditure of time and energy.

Motivation is not something that you do TO people, it is something you do WITH people. Real motivation comes from inside the person, so the motivational teacher, to be truly effective, has to understand, search out, and tap into those already existing motivations. People do not enter the classroom or auditorium with their motivations neutral, blank, and unformed. The fact that they are entering the room—or have arrived at the building—is a result of motivations. It is the height of arrogance to imagine that you are going to take a group of people and, without their participation and consent, motivate them in a direction they do not already want to go. Even accomplished demagogues (Adolf Hitler, Huey Long, and Father Coughlin are notorious 20th-century examples) who seem to mesmerize their audiences, or famous charismatic figures (think of famous politicians, rock stars, or televangelists) are at least partially successful because they are skilled at understanding (and implying their ability to satisfy) the unmet needs clamoring to be fulfilled in the populations they reach.

Consider the students in your classroom. What percentage of them come from families where acceptance into an Ivy League university is the only acceptable measure of school success? Are they being driven by the unrealistic expectations of their parents to compete with fellow students at all cost?

How many of your students suffer from low self-esteem? They accept B or C grades because they believe that's all they are capable of achieving. No one ever told them that they can be stars.

Frank had the opportunity once to counsel a third-grade student who was always getting in trouble. Kreg was a cute kid with dark-brown hair worn long in front touching the brows of his big brown eyes.

Having been sent to the principal's office for the third day in a row, Kreg was asked to meet with Dr. Siccone who was going to help get at the source of the problem. When asked why he got into trouble on such a regular basis, Kreg first said that he was falsely accused of the infraction.

Frank repeated the question as to why Kreg was continuously being sent to the office. His next explanation was that the teacher didn't like him and was just picking on him. Persisting in this line of questioning, Frank once again probed for the underlying cause of the student's frequent misbehavior. Then Kreg said, "Maybe I'm just a bad boy." Frank asked, "Who told you you were a bad boy?" Kreg's response, "My kindergarten teacher." So, three years earlier a teacher had told him he was a bad boy, and he had been acting in accordance with that label ever since.

What labels have been used to describe the students in your classroom by significant adults in their lives, and how have these labels shaped their self-image and motivated their behavior?

GROUPS ARE NEVER HOMOGENEOUS

Any group—students, teachers, salespeople, police, middle managers, church members—is really just a collection of individuals, each carrying his or her own motivations, feelings, personal history, values, concerns, fears, prejudices, hopes, desires, and goals. From this list, you might have noted that people, given a chance to self-select freely, will tend to organize themselves informally and/or formally into groups sharing similar backgrounds, motivations, and values. Depending on their personalities, they will feel more able or less able to differ from their group on the particulars of those values and goals. Yet, given a certain group history, they will tend to share particular attitudes and feelings, hopes and responses. Groups coalesce because they may have to go to the same school, because they live near each other, because they have a common enemy (the feuding gang) or life condition (single parents, members of a minority group), and so on. Within groups, subgroups form and reform as time goes on. And, always, there are loners, newbies, rejects, dissidents, people going through some dramatic life change, or others who do not fit in. All of them are motivated, but by different means toward different ends.

Some are motivated to be there, participate enthusiastically, be a part of the group, class, school, and do their utmost to carry out its goals effectively. Others are motivated to resist parental or school authority or positive peer identification. Some will resist quietly, sullenly, or through nonparticipation. Others choose to resist more actively, even more publicly, sabotaging through a wide variety of techniques such as being extra slow to enter the room, or arriving late, whispering, ostentatiously acting bored, asking irrelevant and/or irreverent questions, and so on. Again, these people are quite motivated, just not in the hoped-for direction. Teachers have to understand the main sets of motivations already existent in groups of students in order to reach them in these admittedly difficult situations. If the teacher resorts to old homilies and what is sometimes called "the common wisdom," the lesson is probably doomed. Appeals to altruism will usually not reach fertile ground. Assuming that everyone in the room is the same as everyone else is a guarantee of failure. The effective motivational teacher must learn about these motivations as they apply to all people in general and then, through research into this specific group of students, how these motivations are at work among them.

The successful motivational teacher, having done his or her homework in terms of researching this particular group, will speak to the various constituencies present in the class, making sure to be inclusive rather than exclusive. The main theme of the lesson may be contrary to the wishes or upsetting to the sensitivities or desires of some subgroups, but, to be successful, the teacher must at least bow toward those groups by acknowledging their concerns and showing them respect. In the best of cases, the motivational teacher will be able to suggest a synthesis in which the needs, views, and concerns of each major subgroup are shown to have common cause with the needs and concerns of the majority.

When the students recognize that you have gone out of your way to find out about them and tailor your teaching directly to their concerns, their receptivity to you and your ideas is markedly increased. Too many students have heard the canned lessons, and they tend to resent having to sit through something so "same-old, same-old." Conversely, they are delighted and grateful when you have made the effort to aim your material accurately, when it is clear that you have personalized and customized your lesson.

One of Frank's most memorable experiences was learning Shakespeare in sophomore English. The contemporary adaptation of *Romeo and Juliet, West Side Story,* was a huge hit at the time. The class was divided into three teams of writers, actors, and directors, each assigned to update one of the Bard's plays. Turning *The Merchant of Venice* into an Elvis Presley–style musical was a bit of a stretch, but Frank—who not only wrote the script but had the lead role—found the chance to be a rock star highly motivating.

HUMAN MOTIVATIONS: THE SHORT LIST

Humans are motivated by a rather extensive list of concerns and needs. Because this is a book about motivational teaching and not a psychological or sociological text, we will explore only a limited number of these motivations, but we will focus on the most significant that can empower the motivational teacher.

There are *physical* needs: water, food, shelter, and so forth. These needs usually (but not always) take precedence over most others. The starving person doesn't think about his self-esteem, for example. The parched person crawling under the desert sun cannot discuss her achievements or the argument she had last year with her supervisor. When students are hungry or have been sitting too long, the motivational teacher is fighting an uphill battle if he or she chooses to continue with the lesson. The class is motivated to go to recess or to the bathroom or to simply move around. A successful motivational teacher doesn't fight the physical needs of the class but does as much as possible to control the classroom environment so that it is conducive to learning.

If you notice your students are experiencing fatigue or low energy, you might ask them to stand and stretch. Consider conducting an organized and humorous stretch session at the beginning of your class complete with music to stretch by. (You might want to use familiar hits such as the music to the dance, *The Macarena*, or James Brown's famous *I Feel Good* song.) This activity actually starts the class off in high energy and a positive mood, and it establishes your personal control over the group and its direction.

There are many other possibilities for dealing with the students' physical needs. For example, you could ask a key question—one that may lie at the core of your ensuing lesson—and then ask each member of your class to pick a nearby partner and stand with his or her partner to discuss their own answers to that key question for two minutes. Make sure they are standing up in order to get some physical movement involved. At the end of that, you've gotten your students awake and energized, as well as having cued them to be thinking about the main issues you're about to teach.

You could ask for two or three volunteers and have them answer a key question or be interviewed by you in the style of Oprah Winfrey and then, based on the answers you receive, begin your lesson in response to their input.

The physiological need for shelter includes the need to be in a space that isn't too hot or cold or humid or dry. Try to motivate a group that's sweltering and falling asleep from the heat! These kinds of environments are really not conducive to learning. Do whatever you can do to prevent human physical needs from being an issue in your classroom.

MASLOW'S HIERARCHY OF HUMAN NEEDS

Abraham Maslow, one of the greatest and most noted psychologists of the 20th century, developed a list of basic human needs. He organized these needs into a *hierarchy*. He felt that certain needs took precedence over others. The physical needs began his list because, when unmet, they tended to block the individual from perceiving or responding to his or her other needs.

Second on Maslow's hierarchy, after physical needs, was *safety*, the need to feel free from imminent danger. If people are convinced that they are in danger, they will not be able to consider anything else. One day, when Hanoch was presenting a workshop at a major hotel in Honolulu, a loud noise and a puff of smoke suddenly came from the PA system amplifier. Smoke kept billowing out. Incredibly, the meeting planner signaled for him to continue. The audience looked startled, and some seemed even frightened. Hanoch asked the audience to get up and leave the room in an orderly fashion. As they were doing so, the smoke alarms went off. As they all went out into the patio, the fire department arrived complete with sirens and men rushing around with hoses.

About an hour and a half later, the fire department allowed the group back into the room. The hotel had brought in a new portable PA system. Hanoch began with a joke about the speaker's hot air triggering the smoke alarms, and the audience laughed. He then asked if everyone felt OK and safe enough to go on. Just asking that question seemed to calm the group, because he was acknowledging publicly their own concerns. Of course, he had ample opportunity for a series of groaners such as, "I'm here to fire you up," "We've really got some hot opportunities," and so on. He asked the audience to help him with the fire jokes, and you can bet they did. It was probably the most interactive keynote address Hanoch had ever done. How would that group have responded had he tried to ignore their safety needs? Safety needs could not be ignored at that moment, nor can they be ignored when planning your lessons, classroom exercise, field trips, and so forth. Safety needs also include needs for peacefulness, security, and lack of danger and threat.

Maslow then adds *belongingness* and *love*. People need affection, inclusion, caring, and relationship with others. When people's need for caring is not met, they can become highly motivated to move toward others. People need to feel they are a part of a family or group, or otherwise have a place, a sense of "at-homeness." They want an identification with the group and its goals and accomplishments. They want to feel loved and worthy of love and affection, friendship, and loyalty. They want to feel connected to significant others. When people feel isolated, unloved or unliked, rejected or excluded, they may become motivated either positively to seek inclusion or negatively to sulk, withdraw, and even seek revenge against those who rejected them. One need only recall the terrible tragedy at Columbine High and other examples of school violence to appreciate the strength of this motivation. Some are motivated to seek inclusion or connectedness but have little or no skills to attain this goal. Their efforts may actually result in more rejection. So powerful are the needs for affection, inclusion, or love that people will often distort themselves out of all recognition in order to fit in or become accepted. No one wants to stand out like a sore thumb or be isolated from the group and unliked by them. This desire to be included, to become part of something bigger than one's self, is one of the most potent needs that the motivational teacher can utilize in reaching a group of students. The motivational teacher can show how students can become more accepted by the group, or conduct an activity that helps them reduce their fear of rejection, or an interactive activity that encourages students to get to know each other better, and this need for relationship and acceptance will feel more fulfilled.

Motivation is important to learning, and feeling valued as a human being is a powerful motivator. Student achievement is enhanced by a school environment that is safe, inviting, and free of harassment. Creating a climate of inclusion in your classroom where students treat each other with mutual respect will pay dividends educationally as well as socially.

A checklist of ideas borrowed from Frank's book, written with Lilia Lopez, *Educating the Heart: Lessons to Build Respect and Responsibility,* is located on the next page.

TEACHER CHECKLIST

Creating a Respectful and Responsible Learning Environment

❑ Am I tailoring my curriculum so that it is relevant to my students, their interests and ambitions, as well as their cultural identity?

❑ Am I aware of my students' various learning styles? Do my teaching strategies reflect this?

❑ Are the books and other materials I use reflective of diversity—ethnicity, culture, race, class, gender, age, handicapping conditions, and so forth?

❑ Are the images on the walls and bulletin boards also reflective of diversity?

❑ Are a variety of family groupings, lifestyles, and types of homes represented in my classroom materials?

❑ Are the materials in my classroom nonsexist, showing both males and females in nurturing roles and depicting a variety of occupational roles and interest areas as being equally appropriate for girls and boys?

❑ How is the seating arrangement consistent with my educational objectives? How does it support all students in learning most effectively?

❑ Have I provided opportunities for my students to help maintain the classroom environment so as to encourage their sense of responsibility?

❑ Were the students involved in developing class rules so that they feel ownership for them?

❑ Do I give my students opportunities to make choices in appropriate areas as a way of letting them exercise responsibility?

❑ Have all my students set goals for themselves? Am I providing effective coaching that may be different for each child but equally empowering for all of them?

After one's needs for inclusion are satisfied, the individual's *self-esteem needs* become predominant. Self-esteem encompasses ideas like self-respect, self-confidence, a sense of one's ability or competence. One of the best authors in the field of self-esteem is our colleague and friend, Dr. Nathaniel Branden. He terms the competence need as the need for *efficacy* or *agency*. People want to feel able to achieve and accomplish as well as feel that they are respected, admired, and valued for their contributions to the group. Personal recognition and prestige are aspects of this need for self-esteem.

Here the motivational teacher finds fertile territory. To publicly celebrate selected individuals for their achievement or contribution to the class makes most students feel good.

Because one of our goals is to have students become more self-motivated and less dependent on external rewards, we encourage you to have your students set goals for themselves. This shifts the focus from pleasing the teacher to applying oneself. When students are acknowledged for achieving one of their goals, the emphasis is on the fact that they succeeded because of their skill and talent, hard work, and commitment. Research shows that when students attribute their success to their efforts rather than to external forces, it increases their self-esteem and leads to future success.

You can ask your students to set goals related to attendance, getting to class on time, following instructions, keeping on task, completing assignments, earning a certain grade, contributing to a canned food drive—any of the areas that are important to individual and team achievement, classroom and school safety and maintenance, and community service.

Maslow's list goes on to what he called the higher needs: *self-actualization*, moving toward the realization of one's potential, growing toward maturity, health, autonomy. Classroom instruction that is designed to mold students into an orderly group capable of sitting still and doing what they are

told for long periods of time runs contrary to the need for
autonomy, maturity, and self-actualization.

On the other hand, helping students assess their strengths
as well as growth areas; allowing them to make informed
choices about what, when, and how they want to study;
encouraging them to monitor their success; and then asking
them to reflect on what they learned about themselves
throughout the process, would contribute greatly to giving
students the self-awareness as well as the tools they need to
be effective lifelong learners.

Maslow then tells us that people's *curiosity needs* come
into play: the desire to know, to learn, to contribute knowledge. A talented motivational teacher will tap into students'
natural curiosity. Ask your students what they are curious
about, what questions they are in search of answers for, what
mysteries they would love to solve, and then design your lesson accordingly. Build some lessons as explorations of
unknown territory rather than as lectures on dry facts.

Then people have *aesthetic needs:* an interest in beauty,
symmetry, rightness, perfection. Design a lesson in which key
concepts are arranged in a symmetrical pattern. Ask your students to apply artistic elements—color, light and dark, balance, harmony, positive tension and resolution, music, surprise, pattern, or repetition—in their work. Give extra credit
for assignments where students have been creative in how
they structured or presented their work.

In school, Frank frequently sought to balance his analytic
skills with his artistic ability and often included a drawing or
other design element in his papers, such as a portrait of
Shakespeare on the cover of his report about the playwright.
He felt more motivated when he was allowed to express his
aesthetic sensibility and was grateful when his teachers

acknowledged him for his effort. Current curriculums based on multiple intelligences and left brain/right brain learning are aimed at satisfying these needs.

Finally, Maslow's hierarchy of human needs has as its pinnacle *transcendent* needs, which include altruism, a developing sense of the unity of all things, intuition, a sense of vision, and a view of the world beyond the narrow focus of one's ego. Community service projects are a great way to involve students in exercising their altruism.

Maslow's famous hierarchy of human needs has great value for the motivational teacher because it points out the areas in which we can reliably assume our students will have great interest. The motivational teacher will also find these additional areas of human need to be of value:

1. *Touch the "heart space,"* those higher values we learned from our parents and spiritual advisors such as love, conscience, altruism, generosity, sharing, sense of rightness. We have an inner voice that speaks to us, to some louder than to others, of what is right, of what is good. When we answer that inner voice, we do feel the best we can ever feel about ourselves. Reminding your students of this voice, while especially avoiding preachiness, can be a powerful tool for motivation.

2. *Sympathy, empathy, and identification* are really strong motivators. *Sympathy* is our tendency to feel similar feelings to the feelings of others. When someone is crying, you may find tears coming to your own eyes. That is sympathy. Any feeling can engender sympathy; infectious laughter is another example. *Empathy* is somewhat different; it happens when you understand and care about someone else's feelings without necessarily experiencing

those feelings yourself. When you say, "Put yourself in this person's place," you are attempting to invoke empathy. Empathy allows us to predict what someone will feel in a given situation. Both of these are examples of the process of *identification*. If you tell your students a story of someone having an unusual and moving experience, you are invoking identification.

Tell your students a story about your own experience, a moment in time when you had a strong feeling about some issue, problem, or concern that they share, or a situation in which you learned something the hard way, and your students are likely to identify with you and get the point memorably.

3. *Achievement, pride, and feelings of competence* are motivations present in everyone: the desire to achieve meaningful accomplishments, to feel pride in one's endeavors, to feel competent or able. They exist in all areas of one's life, from the desire to achieve good relationships with parents and friends, to the desire to do well at school, in sports and hobbies, to be able to be equal with one's classmates in contribution to the group's success. Fill your class with specific, accurate, and dramatic examples of the achievements of the group or its members, and your students will feel motivated. Build into your lessons an opportunity for members of the class to share a success with someone seated nearby, and you'll anchor this powerful motivation with recent positive experience.

4. *Anger, hurt, resentment, and the need for revenge* are the darker side of the human spirit but potent motivations nonetheless. It would be irresponsible and reckless to directly utilize these motivations unless you are attempting to calm these feelings or provide a positive or creative

way for the group to cope with them or resolve them. Here is where the motivational teacher can talk about the redemptive and healing power of forgiveness. You can help students explore how holding on to anger and resentment steals our own energy and distracts us from using our talents most effectively. Two of the most effective motivational teachers on this topic are Dr. Sidney Simon and Suzanne Simon, whose book *Forgiveness* remains a classic "must-read" on this topic. The book has helped many people transcend impacted negative feelings to reach new levels of growth and achievement once they've abandoned the need for revenge and ceased carrying the heavy baggage of unresolved anger. Conflict management programs now taught at many schools are another excellent example of teaching students how to deal with their anger and hurt in a responsible manner.

5. *Competitiveness and the desire for excellence* can be compelling motivations for most people, except those who have already given up, who see no hope for themselves, or who believe the adversary is too powerful to overcome. Most people, at least in our society, seem to have feelings of competitiveness. We have the tendency to compare ourselves to others, to published standards, or to our own past levels of achievement. For sports fans, athletic competition keeps this aspect of their lives stirred up and somewhere near the surface. Closely related to competitiveness is our desire for excellence, our need to become more than merely adequate at what we do. Many areas of human endeavor offer reinforcement for this desire: awards, prizes, standards, seals of approval, tests of significance as well as symbols such as Olympic gold medals and *The Guinness Book of World Records*. Show

your students the path to excellence, and then challenge
them to take it. Teach students to compete with their *own*
last, best achievements.

6. *Fear and the need to resolve it* are another way of expressing
   what Maslow called the *safety* need. You can remind your
   students of the dangers they are in or might someday be
   in and point out how they can conquer those dangers
   through preparation or commitment. This is, again, one
   of the darker motivational forces and, as such, brings with
   it those dangers we've discussed. When reminding people
   about dangers, you run big risks of demotivating them, of
   restimulating their fears to the point of their decision to
   take no action, withdraw, or become depressed or phobic.
   Many people, faced with continuous or overwhelming
   threat, return to old, safe areas of behavior. Even though
   those behaviors may be no help in solving their current
   problems, this retreat helps them feel safer. Triggering
   such a retreat is not what you want to accomplish. If,
   however, the fears are already there and topmost on students' minds, then confronting those fears and offering a
   path toward their resolution makes a great deal of sense.
   A mutual friend of ours, and an excellent motivational
   teacher, is Jack Canfield. Frank and Jack coauthored a
   book entitled *101 Ways to Develop Student Self-Esteem and
   Responsibility.* One of the activities in the book invites students to face their fears by recognizing that "FEAR" stands
   for Fantasized Experiences Appearing Real—the point
   being that most of the time what we are afraid of is some
   imagined future that has not yet happened. Often, just by
   recognizing that you are worrying about something that
   is not yet available to you to do anything about is enough
   to resolve the fear. It is also helpful to focus on what you
   can do *now* to prevent the imagined future from actually
   happening. For example, if my fear is that I am going to

flunk next week's test, then my time is better spent studying for it rather than worrying about it.

7. *Adventure, curiosity, excitement, change, risk, and danger* can be powerful motivators. When people are bored because they've been doing the same things for a very long time, or because they're at the top and there seem to be no new mountains to climb, they begin to crave adventure, excitement, and change.

We believe there are three levels at which most people operate: *the survival level*, where they are using almost all their energy just to get through the day's challenges; *the maintenance level*, where they use a middling level of energy to survive and have some energy left over to repair or plan for repairing things that have gone wrong, or decide how to prevent problems from occurring; and *the enhancement level*, in which they begin to actively seek new challenges, learn new skills.

You can utilize this desire to grow, or, as they used to say in the *Star Trek* series, "to boldly go where no one has gone before." As with all motivation, this one works only with students who are ready to be challenged. Although there are always some few individuals who are unable to reach this level, there are many times when most of the class is really craving a change, a chance to be different, an opportunity to test themselves against the new mountain. If you use this with students who are down at the survival or maintenance levels, they will look at you either blankly or with genuine hostility when you exhort them to gear up for climbing that new peak. This is a good reason to provide several alternative learning strategies—some for the enhancement-level students, some for those on the maintenance level, and extra help for those at survival.

8. *Use humor, fun, playfulness, and lightness.* The human animal likes to laugh. We simply cannot be serious all the

time. There is a need to lighten things up at all times, but when the situation is perilous or tense, the need for humor can become very strong. By interspersing well-chosen humor in your lessons or involving your students in humorous activities or strategies, you utilize this need as one of the engines to propel your motivational message. Schools can be stressful places for students. Being pressured to conform to school rules and teacher expectations, studying for exams and working hard to get good grades, worrying about fitting in with peer groups—all take their toll. Elements of fun and playfulness can help ease the tension and refresh the spirit. The desire to engage again in the educational process is renewed.

Humor works to lower anxiety, release tension, and reduce the psychological distance between people. Once you've laughed with someone, it is harder to be alienated from him or her. Humor can make others seem more approachable and sympathetic. It is critically important that humor be positive and not bitter, discriminatory, racist, sexist, or otherwise involving put-downs and the diminishment of others. Find humor that, if it pokes fun, does so gently. Humor that lasts is the kind that releases the tensions in human situations that we all have experienced—humor that finds the situation funny, that reminds us when we've gotten too caught up in our own egos. Deliberately build humor into your planning for lessons.

USING THE HUMAN MOTIVATIONS

These are the human motivations you can tap as a motivational teacher. This list is intended to begin your search for your own keys to human motivations. As you plan your lesson, ask yourself these questions:

1. What human needs, motives, desires, or concerns are at work in my students? How do I know that? How can I confirm that?
2. What needs and concerns are implied by my subject matter, or by the situation in which my students find themselves?
3. Are there subgroups that have special concerns or needs that must be acknowledged in my classroom?
4. What do I know (or can I find out) that can help these students move toward the satisfaction of those needs?
5. What experiences do I have with similar situations or similar motivations in my own life that I can use as examples and use to help myself empathize with my students?

BIBLIOGRAPHY

Aggeart, Leona. *Anger Management for Youth: Stemming Aggression and Violence.* Bloomington, IN: National Education Service, 1994.

Algozzine, Bob. *50 Simple Ways to Make Teaching More Fun.* Longmont, CO: Sopris West, 1996.

Algozzine, Bob, and James Ysseldyke. *Simple Ways to Make Teaching Math More Fun.* Longmont, CO: Sopris West, 1994.

Arch, David. *Tricks 4 Trainers.* San Francisco: Jossey-Bass Publishers, 1993.

Arch, David. *Tricks 4 Trainers, Vol. II.* San Francisco, Jossey-Bass Publishers, 1993.

Blakely, James, et al. *How the Platform Professionals Keep 'Em Laughin'.* Houston, TX: Rich Publishing Co., 1987.

Blumenfeld, Esther, and Lynne Alpern. *The Smile Connection: How to Use Humor in Dealing with People.* New York: Prentice-Hall, 1986.

Canfield, Jack, and Frank Siccone. *101 Ways to Develop Student Self-Esteem and Responsibility.* Boston: Allyn and Bacon, 1993.

Caroselli, Marlene. *Great Session Openers, Closers, and Energizers: Quick Activities for Warming Up Your Audience.* New York: McGraw-Hill, 1998.

Christian, Sandy Stewart. *Instant Icebreakers: 50 Powerful Catalysts for Group Interaction*. Minneapolis, MN: Whole Person Associates, 1997.

Curwin, Richard L., and Allen Mendler. *Discipline with Dignity*. Alexandria, VA: Association for Supervision and Curriculum Development, 1999.

Droz, Marilyn, and Lori Ellis. *Laughing while Learning: Using Humor in the Classroom*. Longmont, CO: Sopris West, 1996.

Garland, Ron. *Making Work Fun: Doing Business with a Sense of Humor*. San Diego, CA: Shamrock Press, 1991.

Goodman, Joel, and Irv Furman. *Magic and the Educated Rabbit: 360 Magical Motivators for Teachers and Students*. Paoli, PA: Instructo-McGraw-Hill, 1981.

Green, Lila. *Making Sense of Humor: How to Add Joy to Your Life*. Manchester, CT: KIT Publisher, 1993.

Henley, Martin. *Teaching Self Control: Curriculum for Responsible Behavior*. Bloomington, IN: National Education Service, 1997.

Kushner, Malcolm. *The Light Touch: How to Use Humor for Business Success*. New York: Simon and Schuster, 1990.

Loomans, Diane, and Karen Kolberg. *The Laughing Classroom: Everyone's Guide to Teaching with Humor and Play*. Tiburon, CA: H. J. Kramer, 1993.

Metcalf, C. W., and Roma Felible. *Lighten Up: Survival Skills for People Under Pressure*. Reading, MA: Addison-Wesley, 1992.

Michelli, Joseph. *Humor, Play and Laughter: Stress-Proofing Life with Your Kids*. Golden, CO: Love and Logic Press, 1998.

Robertson, Jeanne. *Humor: The Magic of Genie*. Houston, TX: Rich Publishing, 1990.

Rose, Ed. *Presenting and Training with Magic: 53 Tricks You Can Use to Energize Any Audience*. New York: McGraw-Hill, 1998.

Scannell, Edward, and John Newstrom. *The Big Book of Presentation Games*. New York: McGraw-Hill, 1998.

Seligman, Martin E. R. *Learned Optimism: How to Change Your Mind and Your Life*. New York: Simon and Schuster, 1990.

Siccone, Frank, and Lilia Lopez. *Educating the Heart: Lessons to Build Respect and Responsibility*. Boston: Allyn and Bacon, 2000.

Simon, Sidney B., and Suzanne Simon. *Forgiveness: How to Make Peace with Your Past and Get on with Your Life*. New York: Warner Books, 1991.

Weinstein, Matt. *Managing to Have Fun: How Fun at Work Can Motivate Your Employees.* New York: Simon and Schuster, 1996.

Weinstein, Matt, and Joel Goodman. *Playfair: Everybody's Guide to Non-Competitive Play.* San Luis Obispo, CA: Impact Publishers, 1986.

West, Edie. *201 Icebreakers: Group Mixers, Warm-Ups, Energizers, and Playful Activities.* New York: McGraw-Hill, 1996.

Wilson, Steve. *The Art of Mixing Work and Play.* Columbus, OH: Applied Humor Systems, Inc., 1992.

3

WHAT IS A
MOTIVATIONAL
TEACHER?

On the first day of school, a teacher was glancing over the
roll when she noticed a number after each student's name,
such as 154, 136, or 142.

"Wow! Look at these IQs," she said to herself. "What a ter-
rific class." The teacher promptly determined to work harder
with this class than with any other she ever had.

Throughout the year, she came up with innovative lessons
that she thought would challenge the students, because she
didn't want them to get bored with work that was too easy.

Her plan worked! The class outperformed all the other classes
that she taught in the usual way.

Then, during the last quarter of the year, she discovered
what those numbers after the students' names really were:
their locker numbers.

CHARACTERISTICS OF A MOTIVATIONAL LESSON

Every lesson should be motivational in that the teacher should have presented important, relevant, and fresh information in a way that piques the students' interest and leaves them wanting to remember the information and use it in their lives. Having said that, we must admit that many teachers fail to match that model, but, from the point of view of the students, they certainly wished they had! The students, you see, are really on your side. They don't want to be bored or disappointed. They would much rather that you succeed. They'd love it if today's class is fun, fast-paced, and fascinating.

The lesson that we label "motivational," and that is designed or intended to be motivational, has certain unique characteristics that differentiate it from lessons that are designed to impact information or develop skills.

The Need for Inspiration

The motivational lesson should have the quality of *inspiration:* of presenting information, ideas, themes, concepts, or information with the goal of increasing the listener's motivation, which we define as *the desire and intention to do particular things, achieve certain goals, take on specific attitudes, begin desired processes and procedures.* Motivational lessons differ from all others in that they are *deliberately designed to induce motivation.* Other lessons may be *incidentally* motivating, but the motivational lesson is so by design and intent.

An informative lesson can be motivational because people do feel more positively disposed toward topics about which they feel they have enough information to be confident and comfortable. If the information they receive has the character of being shocking, unexpected, or frightening, or implies some problem that needs resolution, the students can be motivated even if the teacher fails to draw the moral and urge action. Speaking to a group of parents and letting them know about planned cuts in funding for a valued reading-enhancement program may produce strong and even unintended motivation. A lesson designed to help build skills—for example, a computer class that teaches students how to send e-mails to fellow students in another part of the world—may produce motivation in the group, because as they feel more likely to succeed, they will be more willing and even eager to try out what they learned. Many kinds of lessons can have as a collateral or side effect the motivation of the students. But only the motivational lesson has been deliberately and knowingly planned to have this effect.

Motivational lessons do not have only one possible format or only a limited number of styles and techniques. It is possible to design a motivational lesson that uses as its main propulsive force humor, personal stories, shocking facts and exposés, or that appeals to patriotism, loyalty, friendship, or any number of emotions. The essence of the motivational lesson is in its intended outcome: human motivation. *If the lesson is a catalyst for a commitment by the students toward the desired goals, it is motivational, whatever its content, style, or technique.*

Your Own Belief Is the Key

In ancient Rome, a respected senator from an old and powerful patrician family, Cato the Elder, rose to speak in the Senate one day, as was his right and privilege. When he was recognized by the Speaker, he simply said, *"Cartago delenda est!"* [Carthage must be destroyed!], and promptly sat down, to the consternation and confusion of the other senators. Some tittered, others muttered in derision. At that time,

Carthage was a trading partner and competitor of Rome but certainly not its enemy. In fact, many Roman families had important financial ties and business interests in Carthage. When he was asked to explain, Cato the Elder said nothing. His remarks were dismissed as an aberration. The next day, Cato rose again and demanded the floor. Again, when recognized, he declared in ringing tones, "*Cartago delenda est!*" Again, there were derisive whispers and a few laughs. Most did not want to offend his powerful family and remained silent. The Senate just went on with its business without further comment.

Every day, for nearly three years, Cato rose and spoke his famous line, "*Cartago delenda est!*" Incredulity turned to open hostility and derision. Taunting, teasing, loud hostile commentary became the norm for a while. But the power of Cato's consistency, of his steadfastness in the face of ridicule, of the certitude with which he spoke, began to erode the opposition. Gradually, almost imperceptibly, senators began to view news of Carthage with suspicion. Otherwise ordinary events were now viewed through a new lens and interpreted as possible support for Cato's position. Almost three years later, the Roman Senate unanimously voted to declare war on Carthage. In the war that ensued, Carthage was indeed destroyed, and Rome's main competitor in the Mediterranean was no more. Rome gained immeasurably from this conflict, started by one man, with one simple insistent message. That is the power of a motivational message. In this case, its length was unimportant; Cato did not use a chalkboard or an overhead projector, a computerized presentation program, or any worksheets or handouts. His most powerful techniques were repetition and his own unshakable belief in his idea. That belief was translated into his tone of voice, his volume, his nonverbal behavior as he looked majestically around the senate chamber, delivering his one-line peroration.

More recent history is replete with examples giving motivational messages with stunning power, often in wartime. Lincoln's famed "Gettysburg Address" galvanized a nation reeling from one of the most disastrous victories possible. Yes, the Union carried the day at Gettysburg, but at the cost of many thousands dead and wounded. How to repair the fighting spirit of the nation? Following a famous speaker, Edward Everett, who spoke for nearly two-and-a-half hours (the audiences of that day had far more staying power than those of today), Lincoln gave his message in 271 words.*

Fourscore and seven years ago our fathers brought forth upon this continent, a new nation, conceived in Liberty, and dedicated to the proposition that all men are created equal.

Now we are engaged in a great civil war, testing whether that nation, or any nation so conceived, and so dedicated, can long endure. We are met on a great battle-field of that war. We have come to dedicate a portion of that field, as a final resting place for those who here gave their lives, that that nation might live. It is altogether fitting and proper that we should do this.

But, in a larger sense, we can not dedicate—we can not consecrate—we can not hallow—this ground. The brave men, living and dead, who struggled here, have consecrated it, far above our poor power to add or detract. The world will little note, nor long remember, what we say here, but it can never forget what they did here. It is for us the living, rather, to be dedicated

---

* Lincoln wrote out his "Gettysburg Address" six times, all with slight differences. This version is from one of the five existing handwritten copies, which is displayed at the Old State Capitol in Springfield, Illinois.

here to the unfinished work which they who fought here, have, thus far, so nobly advanced. It is rather for us to be here dedicated to the great task remaining before us—that from these honored dead we take increased devotion to that cause for which they here gave the last full measure of devotion—that we here highly resolve that these dead shall not have died in vain—that this nation, under God, shall have a new birth of freedom—and that, government of the people, by the people, for the people, shall not perish from the earth.

It is worth noting that many of the newspaper reporters present did not think much of Lincoln's speech and focused most of their attention and dispatches on Everett's longer and more florid oratory. However, Everett himself, an extremely famous speaker of the day, immediately said that he wished he had given Lincoln's speech. He recognized the greatness in it despite (or maybe partly because of) its brevity.

MOTIVATION IS A COOPERATIVE VENTURE

A motivational lesson does not gain its power by imposing new motivations upon its hearers. It is not likely that a teacher can singly imbue a group of students with motivations with which they did not enter the room. Instead a motivational teacher attempts to uncover, understand, and tap into the motivations already present in the students. Many years ago, in describing children's learning, educators used to say the child's mind was a *tabula rasa*, a blank slate, upon which the teacher writes the lesson. This presumed that children entered school totally blank, empty, devoid of know-

ledge, skills, preferences, abilities, disabilities, and prejudices.
This view of learning seemed to give the teacher even more
enormous power than he or she already has. The teacher sup-
plied all knowledge, all skill, and imbued the children with
all of their attitudes and beliefs about the subject and about
themselves that would enable them to use that knowledge
constructively.

Reality is quite different from this now discredited view of
learning. Children do not enter the schoolroom like blank
tapes waiting to be recorded. Instead, by the time a child
enters kindergarten, he or she has learned (in most cases) to
walk, talk, sing, run, play, and perform many complicated
maneuvers like working a VCR, playing with a computer, and
so on. The child already has tastes ("I hate Brussels sprouts!")
and abilities ("I can get on the Internet and find the Disney
Web page!") as well as learned helplessness in certain areas
("My mom says she can't do math either!") and prejudices
("My dad says it's stupid for boys to have to take home
economics!").

Similarly, your students will walk into the room filled
with their own life experiences, their own points of view, and
systems of values. Before you begin your lesson, they may
have brought in anger or fear. They will be energized or
exhausted, nervous or relaxed, hopeful or hopeless, elated or
depressed, hungry or sated, all with no regard to you and
your plans for them.

Will your lesson really speak to them? Will it touch some
resonant chord in their hearts? It will not do that as a result
of your *telling them* how to feel or how to behave. It can only
work if you've done your homework and discovered who
they are, what issues are on their minds, what history has
helped them feel that way, and what directions seem to make
most sense to them.

Motivation is, therefore, not something one does to someone, but rather it is something one does with them. It is a cooperative venture. People resent being manipulated without their consent. They don't want to be psyched, hypnotized, controlled, dominated, or exploited. They will respond to those attempts with resistance, cynicism, anger, resentment, and hostility. Naked manipulation will rebound and produce the exact opposite to the desired outcome: a group not only not motivated in the direction you've chosen but angry and suspicious of you and, often, school in general. Students, when pushed, often become *reactive*, deliberately behaving in oppositional ways designed to frustrate or sabotage the person pushing them.

Motivation is a cooperative venture! It is your business to discover your students' motivations and their desired goals. If you think their goals are erroneously chosen or need revision, it is necessary for you to build that case for them and involve them cooperatively in seeing the new outcomes you think have more merit. When you touch upon your students' feelings and fears, their hopes and hurts, their experiences and expectations, do so tenderly and respectfully. Make yourself equally vulnerable to them by sharing your own hopes and dreams, your own similar or extraordinary experiences and the processes by which you came to the conclusions you will share with them.

LIGHT YOUR INNER FIRE
IN ORDER TO LIGHT THEIRS

Remember that students *want* to be motivated. They want to be enthralled. They will be grateful to you if you can remind them of why they are there, of how they can restore their old feelings of motivation if those are now lost or faded. They will be delighted if you can restimulate in them an uncritical, unself-conscious, almost naive faith in what they are doing, or what they ought to do, or what they are about to do. They will be relieved if you can help them find pride in their own selves, accomplishments, or actions, for we live in an age of cynicism and self-consciousness. In our busy lives we rush around doing and doing. Sometimes the activity seems to take the place of thought. We may find no time or place for introspection, for thinking through the tough issues or for choosing thoughtfully our life's direction. The motivational teacher who is most successful is one who can nudge us in that direction or who can remind us of the need to take that moment to choose our next steps more wisely. A poster Hanoch has in his office says it best: *A friend is someone who knows your song and sings it to you when you forget.*

Whatever historians may decide about the greatness or ultimate value of John F. Kennedy's presidency, almost all agree that he was a consummately charismatic speaker. His inaugural address touched the hearts of so many of his fellow citizens: " . . . ask not what your country can do for you; ask what you can do for your country." Whatever he accomplished in his brief and fatally interrupted presidency, he managed to sing America's song back to us when it seemed that many had forgotten it. Thousands clamored to join the Peace Corps or engage in other public-spirited works as a result of that single famous motivational message. Want to be a motivational teacher? Find out what your audience's song is, and sing it to them, unashamedly, with spirit and conviction, with flamboyance, and with your own inner fire. Make yourself equally vulnerable by sharing how much of that song is yours, too, and you will have become a motivational teacher!

MOTIVATION AND THE POWER OF PERSUASION

You cannot antagonize and influence at the same time.

J. S. Knox

Advertising agencies spend millions of dollars every year conducting market research on how to motivate consumers to buy products they don't really need. Education, on the other hand, has neither the money nor the mandate to research how to motivate students to learn, even though consuming the information schools have to offer may be much more valuable than consuming what advertisers are selling.

While many teachers may balk at the idea of applying mass-marketing techniques to the more elevated profession of educating students, a quick look at advertising techniques will reveal what excellent teachers have been doing all along.

We suggest reading this with an open mind. Instead of asking yourself, "What does this have to do with my teaching?" ask, "How could I apply this to make my teaching more interesting for me as well as my students?"

1. KNOW YOUR AUDIENCE

The better you know your students, understand their interests, and assess their skill level, the more effective you can be in reaching them and teaching them. The next two chapters will expand on this idea and suggest ways of acquiring important information about your students.

2. GET THEIR ATTENTION

Advertisers use loud music, quick-cut action, celebrity spokespeople, clever animation, and a whole range of other tricks to try to get their message to break through the clutter of the constant bombardment of commercials.

While we are not suggesting that you have the time, money, and skills to compete with television and other forms of entertainment, we are suggesting that using some tricks of the trade to attract your students' attention could be the spark they need to become more engaged in the learning process.

Chapter 7 will discuss "attention-getters" you can use in your classroom, and Chapter 8 is devoted to the power of storytelling.

3. COMMUNICATE BENEFITS IN RELEVANT TERMS

Marketing experts distinguish between a product's features and its benefits. A *feature* describes an aspect of the product— for example, four-wheel drive, antilock brakes, or convertible top. A *benefit*, on the other hand, translates the feature into a value proposition from the user's perspective—for example, an opportunity for adventure, confidence that your family will be safe, an experience of fun and freedom. The more you can establish a link between what you are teaching and how it is relevant for your students, the more motivated they will be to learn the information and/or acquire the skills. In Chapter 9 you will learn more about how to construct your lessons so that the benefits of education will be more relevant and, hence, more motivating to your students.

4. BE PERSUASIVE

By definition, to motivate is to persuade someone to act. Advertisers use a number of different persuasive techniques to get people to believe in the benefits of their products. Some of the most familiar are:

■ *Celebrity spokesperson.* If you like Rosie O'Donnell and believe she wouldn't lie to you and your kids, then you can take her word for the quality and value you will find at the store she is pitching.

CLASSROOM VERSION: Use this as an opportunity to develop your students' critical thinking skills. Have them write an essay on which celebrities are used to try and sell products to their age group. Ask them if they find these ads persuasive. Why or why not?

■ *Proof by agreement.* "Nine out of ten doctors recommend this preparation," therefore it must be effective.

CLASSROOM VERSION: Make posters with pictures of your students advocating studying the binomial theorem. Have student volunteers make TV commercials for things you are studying.

■ *Proof by demonstration.* Show how the product works, usually by simulation. The medicine prevents heartburn by coating your stomach, as shown in this drawing. "Makes sense. Works for me."

CLASSROOM VERSION: Try to find ways of making learning concrete—make it tangible, hands-on. Try it, do it, experiment.

■ *The proof of the pudding is in the eating.* The before and after testimonials by real people like yourself who lost 10 pounds through this program can be very convincing.

CLASSROOM VERSION: Have student volunteers do audio or video interviews with satisfied customers—students from former years who feel they benefited from learning this material.

■ *Proof by personality.* Building a brand personality is something on which corporations spend an enormous amount of time, energy, and intelligence. Johnson & Johnson considers their company name to be not just a trademark, but a "trust mark." As the maker of baby products, they recognize the importance of maintaining an image of safe, gentle, caring, no-more-tears products.

A brand personality is a relationship between the company and the consumers. When a company that has created a strong brand with one product releases another product with the same brand name, the value associated with the brand is transferred to the new product. Disney, for example, went from cartoons to full-length features, theme parks, and retail stores.

CLASSROOM VERSION: You appear on the poster or in the video reminding the class about a previous lesson they enjoyed, and saying, "If you liked _____, you'll *love* _____."

■ *Proof positive.* Most ad campaigns focus on the positive benefits of purchasing the products being sold. Some, however, imply negative consequences, like the famous ads that focus on how dry your peanut-butter-and-jelly-sandwich will be if you forget to pick up milk on the way home.

CLASSROOM VERSION: Have your students do an Internet-based research project. Checking out corporate Web sites, they could ask company executives to respond to the query, "If getting a good education is the 'product,' what evidence do they have that it works." Invite successful business people to make the connection between something they learned in school and how they applied it to their careers.

What are the traditional methods schools use to motivate students? What can we learn from marketing communications strategies that could be used to persuade students to apply themselves, make the effort, achieve their educational goals? Additional persuasive presentation tools are included in Chapter 10.

5. MAKE IT MEMORABLE

The basic idea here is to keep the message of the advertising alive in the viewer's mind long after the 30-second spot is over. Some typical techniques are listed below along with some ideas at the top of the next page on how you can apply these to your teaching.

■ *Catchy jingles.* Have you ever found yourself replaying in your mind a commercial message—for example, "I don't wanna grow up . . ."

CLASSROOM VERSION: Remind students of how the "ABCs" song helped them learn the alphabet, and then hold a contest where teams of students write songs or jingles to help the class remember a set of facts they need to learn.

■ *Clever slogans or tag lines.* Some of these become part of everyday vernacular: "Where's the beef?" "Just do it," "Whatsup?"

CLASSROOM VERSION: Assign students the task of finding slogans that were used throughout history and give an oral report on the meaning and historical significance of the motto. For example, "Remember the Alamo!" or "The New Deal."

■ *Repetition.* Say it often enough, and people will remember it no matter how obnoxious. "Don't squeeze the Charmin" comes to mind. And, of course, "Carthage must be destroyed!"

CLASSROOM VERSION: Select something you want your students to memorize, such as, "I comes before e, except after c." and repeat it at the beginning of class each day for a week.

■ *Element of surprise.* The battery-operated bunny showing up in what seemed to be another commercial is an example of this technique.

CLASSROOM VERSION: On a day that the students have prepared to take a test, surprise them with the announcement that you have postponed the test until the next class. After their sighs of relief and applause of gratitude, do a stress-free activity—a project you know your students will enjoy.

▪ *Humor.* The clever, self-deprecating wit of the Volkswagen Beetle advertising back in the 1960s completely changed the brand image of that car from ugly to hip. This legacy continues with the ad campaign being used to reintroduce the VW Beetle to today's market.

CLASSROOM VERSION: Collect cartoons and comic strips that are appropriate to your students' age group. Use one of the cartoons to add some humor to your introduction to a new lesson or at the end of a class period. This works best if the cartoon reinforces the point you are making.

▪ *Exaggeration.* Stretching cheese from room to room makes the point about how generous the toppings are on this type of pizza.

CLASSROOM VERSION: Do a lesson on hyperbole and have the students write a paper where they describe an event that happened to them. Instruct them to deliberately exaggerate the truth in order to create an effect. Extend the learning by looking for the use of hyperbole in works of poetry and discussing with your students how this device is used for literary purposes.

▪ *Likeable characters.* Poppin' Fresh, the Dough Boy; Tony the Tiger; the Taco Bell chihuahua; Michael Jordan; Bugs Bunny—to name a few—captured the attention of audiences.

CLASSROOM VERSION: Probably the best application of this motivation tool is to be likeable yourself. Being likeable doesn't mean always pleasing your students, being easy on them, or trying to be their friends; it does mean being positive, approachable, and encouraging.

5 KNOW YOUR STUDENTS

A gossip is one who talks to you about others;
a bore is one who talks to you about himself; and
a brilliant person is one who talks to you about yourself.

Anonymous

Let's look at ways in which advertising techniques can
become part of the motivational teacher's tool kit. How well
do you know your students, and how can you use that information to build a stronger link between what you need to
teach and what they want to learn?

Teaching is communication. Communication requires a
shared context or frame of reference in order for the meaning
of the delivered communication to be received accurately. In
order to teach your students, you need to be able to communicate with them. In order to communicate with them, you
need to understand their frame of reference.

In advertising, product messages are shaped by both
demographics—age, gender, cultural heritage, geographic loca-
tion, and the like, as well as by psychographics—the mindset
of the intended audience, including expectations, hopes, and
dreams; and problems, concerns, fears, and insecurities.

Besides the general information about age-appropriate
teaching methodologies, what more do you or can you know
about your students? Frank worked recently with a charter

school in Sonoma County, north of San Francisco. The school has a strong student-centered philosophy. The staff believes it is important for students to have choices regarding their education so that they are more involved and accept greater responsibility. A student survey is used to help teachers know areas of high interest around which they can build thematic teaching units. The basics of math, language arts, science, and so on are taught in the context of a project where the students are involved as active learners.

The difference between talking about a product and selling a product is the difference between teaching a subject and teaching students. Understanding your students also involves appreciating their different learning styles, which will be covered in greater detail in the next chapter.

Some of the questions you might want to get your students to answer are:

- What are the things you think an "educated adult" needs to know?

- What are your interests, hobbies, favorite ways to spend time?

- What are your skills, talents, things you do well, things you enjoy doing?

- What is your favorite:
  - subject in school?
  - type of food?
  - music?
  - TV program?
  - book?
  - movie?
  - sport or type of physical activity?

- thing to do with friends?
- thing to do with family?
- thing to do alone?

■ What careers have you considered?

■ What skills would you need to learn in order to be successful?

■ How do you picture your life when you are 30 years old?

■ If you were in charge of what students are required to learn in school, what subjects would you include?

■ What is stupid about school?

■ What is smart about school?

■ Who has a job that you think you would like to do?

■ How do you get money?

■ On what do you spend money?

■ What are your strongest dislikes? Pet peeves?

■ What do you worry about the most?

A parent/guardian survey or conference could also yield valuable information that you can use in tailoring your curriculum to make it more accessible to your students. It has been said that "students don't care what you know until they know you care."

You can show you care by integrating your understanding of who they are and what matters to them in the examples you give to illustrate a point; by the pictures you post on bulletin boards in the classroom, reflecting images to which your students can relate; and by the supplemental materials you provide to add texture to the standard texts.

6 MOTIVATION AND LEARNING STYLES

Teaching is something that takes place only when learning
does. No matter what teachers are doing in their classes, if
students are not learning something significant, they are not
teaching. When students fail, teachers have failed more.

Michael Niflis

So far, we have been discussing motivating students from the
viewpoint of how you present the material. This, of course, is
only half the equation. How students receive or process information is the other important component to be considered.

There are a number of different approaches to understanding student learning styles. What they all have in common is an appreciation for the fact that not all students learn
in the same way. In order to be an effective teacher, you need
to include multiple modes or modalities so that each student
has an opportunity to grasp the meaning of your message.
This chapter presents a model for learning styles based on
Myers-Briggs Personality Types.

Throughout history, people have sought ways to understand and explain human behavior. The ancient Greeks developed a system for characterizing individuals into four tem-
peraments: melancholic, choleric, sanguine, and phlegmatic.
American Plains Indians used the directions of the compass to
describe specific behavior types: north was innocent, south
meant wisdom, east stood for imagination, and the quality of
the west was introspection.

In 1921, the Swiss psychiatrist Carl Gustav Jung wrote *Psychological Types,* in which he described four basic personality styles: intuitor, thinker, feeler, and sensor. Building upon Jung's theoretical model, two American women, Katharine Briggs and her daughter, Isabel Briggs Myers, developed a system using four personality preference scales and 16 distinct personality types. The Myers-Briggs Type Indicator® (MBTI)* is now one of the most widely used psychological instruments. Its reliability and validity have been well documented from hundreds of scientific studies conducted over the past 40 years.

The four Myers-Briggs personality preference scales— Extravert/Introvert, Sensor/Intuitive, Thinker/Feeler, Judger/Perceiver—are summarized in the following charts.

PERSONALITY PREFERENCES

E (Extraverts)	I (Introverts)
■ Talk first, think later	■ Think before speaking
■ Find listening difficult	■ Perceived as good listeners
■ Like to involve many people	■ Enjoy time alone
■ Tend to dominate a conversation	■ Think "talk is cheap"
■ Prefer to generate ideas in a group and enjoy meetings as an opportunity to express an opinion	■ Have few close confidants
■ Capable of doing many things at once	■ Prefer not to be interrupted
■ Seem easily approachable and need affirmation from others	■ Appear shy, reserved, reflective

*The Myers-Briggs Type Indicator and MBTI are registered trademarks of Consulting Psychologists Press.

S (Sensors)	N (Intuitives)
■ Prefer specific answers to specific questions	■ Tend to give general answers to questions
■ Would rather *do* something than *think* about it	■ Have vivid imaginations and are consistently exploring future possibilities
■ Concentrate on what they are doing at the moment	■ Like complexity and think about several things at once
■ Work better with facts and figures than with ideas and theories and with things presented sequentially rather than randomly	■ Find details, including budgets and timelines, to be boring
■ Enjoy jobs that yield tangible results	■ Enjoy figuring out how things work just for the pleasure of it
■ Take things literally and subscribe to the notion that "seeing is believing"	■ Seek meaning, connections, and interrelatedness behind things

T (Thinkers)	F (Feelers)
■ Stay cool, calm, and objective	■ Apply values and subjective criteria when making a decision
■ Settle disputes based on what is fair and truthful rather than on what will make people happy	■ Take people's feelings into account
■ Seek clarity rather than harmony	■ Prefer harmony over clarity

PERSONALITY PREFERENCES (continued)

T (Thinkers) (continued)	**F (Feelers)** (continued)
■ Able to make difficult decisions based on logic	■ Seek to accommodate the needs of others
■ Think it is more important to be right than to be liked	■ Avoid conflict, want people to get along
■ Believe things that are logical and scientific and remember numbers and figures more readily than faces and names	■ Empathize with others and are concerned with the impact on people

J (Judgers)	**P (Perceivers)**
■ Keep lists and use them	■ Prefer being spontaneous rather than working from a plan
■ Thrive on order, systems, structure	■ Love to explore the unknown
■ Think schedules and deadlines are important	■ Often wait until the last minute to get something done
■ Like to work things to completion and according to plan	■ Tend to be tentative, maintaining a wait-and-see attitude to keep options open; don't like to be pinned down
■ Prefer to be in control, where things are decided and fixed	■ Are flexible and adaptable

Our personalities are made up of some degree of each of these dimensions. Typically, we each show a preference—it may be a slight, moderate, or strong preference—for one end of the spectrum over the other. What is important to realize about this is that certain types of classroom activities and structures work better for some students than for others. It is essential that you vary your teaching methodologies to account for the learning style requirements of all of your students.

For example, students who are extraverts, given their tendency to think out loud and become energized by working in groups, will learn best through class discussions, whereas a student who is more introverted would prefer to work independently and respond in writing. With some effort on your part, you may be able to get an introverted student to take a more active part during group interactions, and you may be able to get the extraverts in your room to sit still and be quiet. But you need to know that neither of these comes naturally.

Students who are sensors learn best when the material is presented in a logical, sequential, step-by-step manner. They need practical examples, hands-on demonstrations, and concrete, tangible results. They tend to be detail-oriented and good with facts and figures. Material that is too abstract, theoretical, or philosophical will be over their heads. Questions for which there is one right answer work well with these students.

On the other end of this continuum are intuitive learners. In contrast to their sensory counterparts, intuitives get bored if the material is too detail-oriented. They are more comfortable when they understand the larger purpose and can see the reasoning behind an assignment. Because they enjoy finding connections and relationships among things, they are adept at using metaphors and analogies. Presenting information in the form of charts and graphs is an effective way to teach your students who are Intuitive.

The third dimension assessed by the Myers-Briggs Type Inventory—the difference between a Thinker and a Feeler—is revealed most clearly in how people make decisions. Thinkers are more likely to be persuaded by reason, objective data, quantitative research—"Just the facts, ma'am." (*Dragnet*'s Sergeant Joe Friday was definitely a Thinker.) Feelers tend to be more empathetic and would consider the effect any decision would have on the people involved. Personal values and subjective judgments are strong motivators for Feeler types.

If you want history to be meaningful to your students who are Thinkers, tell them in what years a war began and ended, how many people were killed in the war, and how much it cost to rebuild that nation's economy. To bring the same events to life for Feelers, have them read biographical accounts of people who lived during those times so your students can share in their actual experiences.

The biggest difference between a Judger and a Perceiver is that the Judger has a picture in mind of how the world should be and works toward bringing this plan to reality. A Perceiver is more opportunistic and takes advantage of what the world presents rather than trying to get it to conform to a preconceived image.

Because Judgers are comfortable in a structured environment, they do well in classrooms where they know what to expect: classes begin and end on time; certain routines have been established; and systems are in place to keep things organized, orderly, and under control. Most schools do not accommodate Perceivers very well. They are flexible, adaptable, spontaneous, and creative. Often waiting until the last minute to get things done, Perceivers avoid making commitments because they like to keep their options open.

Frank observed a third-grade teacher who developed a method for balancing structure and spontaneity. Each morning he would write the day's schedule on the chalkboard, indicating what subjects would be covered during which time periods. He would always include a free period during which the students could choose from a range of options.

The first step in motivating students through learning styles is to know your own personality preferences. How do you learn best? Are you more outgoing or reserved, concrete or abstract, structured or spontaneous, teaching from the mind or the heart? Once you know your natural inclinations, you can then focus on expanding your comfort level in other dimensions in order to be able to connect with each of your students.

Next, you should learn as much as you can about your students and their preferred style of interacting with information and acquiring knowledge. This way you can teach to their strengths and improve the likelihood of their success.

Finally, in planning your lessons and structuring your classroom environment, you should seek to accommodate a diverse range of learning styles and modalities. The following charts will serve as useful checklists for you.

For your students who are *Extraverts:*

❏ They tend to be very outgoing and like to talk a lot. Provide ample time for class discussion, as well as opportunities for presenting, demonstrating, explaining, and performing.

❏ Thinking out loud is a common characteristic of extraverts, so give these students time to talk through their answer to your question. Writing assignments should allow for rough drafts, and other projects should encourage trial-and-error experimentation.

❏ Cooperative learning and other group activities work well. Physical movement and learning by interacting is preferred.

❏ Extraverts get their energy from outside forces and hence are susceptible to external influences. Looking good in public is important to them. So if you need to correct them, do so privately. (This is actually good advice for all students regardless of their personality.)

❏ While they can be encouraged to sit still and be quiet, it doesn't come naturally.

For your students who are *Introverts:*

❏ Introverts are typically not comfortable speaking in public. If you want an opinion or answer from these students, you will probably have to ask or give them an alternative way to respond more privately.

❏ These students prefer to think before speaking. Allow time for them to process their answers by themselves before calling upon them. Better yet, give them the questions in writing beforehand so that they can prepare on their own.

❏ They are not likely to perform well in group settings. One-on-one works better. Give them the choice of what work products to display publicly and what to keep private.

❏ Allow quiet time for them to study without interruption. They learn best when they can listen, observe, and reflect.

❏ Invite them to put their thoughts and feelings in writing with enough time to edit and polish their thoughts before sharing.

❏ While they can be encouraged to participate more in class, it doesn't come naturally.

For your students who are *Sensors:*

❑ Sensors take things literally, so when giving an assignment, use language that is clear, specific, and precise. They expect to be taught directly rather than through some discovery method.

❑ Answer their questions with specific answers rather than general comments. They prefer to know exactly what's expected of them before they start to work.

❑ Sensors learn best when provided with facts and figures. Provide them with experiences that engage as many of the senses as possible.

❑ If you want them to understand the subject matter, present it in a logical, sequential, step-by-step manner. They are good at memorizing details.

❑ Use practical examples; hands-on demonstrations; and concrete, tangible manipulatives to promote learning. Start with solid, familiar facts and move sequentially toward the more abstract.

❑ Material that is too abstract, philosophical, or theoretical will be over their heads.

For your students who are *Intuitives:*

❑ Put the current lesson in context for these students. Explain the purpose, how it fits in to what they have already learned, and how it relates to future lessons.

❑ Use charts and graphs, whenever possible, to deepen their understanding.

❑ These students are likely to appreciate abstract concepts. (New math was probably created by an Intuitive.) Start your lesson with something novel and different to spark their interest.

❑ In science they would gravitate to possibility theories; in history, big ideas and grand visions (e.g., Manifest Destiny) will capture their imagination.

❑ Expect their writing to be poetic and metaphoric rather than literal. They value opportunities to do original, inventive work.

❑ Memorizing factual information will not be their forte.

For your students who are *Thinkers:*

❑ These students are much more comfortable in the cognitive rather than the affective domain. They find objective data more persuasive than subjective arguments. Subject matter should be constructed in a logical manner.

❑ They will respect you if you are truthful and treat them fairly. Thinkers care what you know and don't need to know you care.

❑ Present information clearly, efficiently, and accurately. Be brief, concise, and to the point. Give them interesting problems to analyze.

❑ They are likely to thrive in a traditional academic environment that is intellectually stimulating. The classroom should be well organized in logical systems.

❑ While Thinkers can be encouraged to "get in touch with their feelings" and to practice "empathetic listening," these won't come naturally.

For your students who are *Feelers:*

❑ These students do best when they are engaged emotionally, when they feel a human connection with their teacher and classmates.

❏ A warm, caring, harmonious environment is important to their feeling comfortable.

❏ Feelers respond to teachers who are friendly, personalized, supportive, and appreciative.

❏ If you invest time in listening to these students and responding to their needs, they will work hard for you out of a sense of loyalty.

❏ Self-esteem activities, team-building exercises, conflict management training, social and extracurricular events all make school life more meaningful for these students.

❏ While they can be encouraged to be more rational and not take things personally, these won't come naturally.

For your students who are *Judgers:*

❏ Make sure your lesson plan is organized with a clear, easy-to-understand structure.

❏ Classroom rules need to be clearly defined and consistently maintained.

❏ Provide opportunities for these students to be in control, such as running class meetings or being a team leader on a cooperative learning project.

❏ These students work best in an environment that is well organized, where schedules are maintained, materials and supplies are properly stored, and everything functions in an orderly fashion.

❏ Give assignments that have clear instructions, beginning and ending dates, and explicit performance objectives. Celebrate completions.

❏ Tests with unambiguous questions where there is only one right answer work best for students who are judgers.

For your students who are *Perceivers:*

❏ Too much structure will seem overly confining. Keeping these students engaged will require a willingness on your part to be flexible and adaptable.

❏ Break up classroom routines with creative and spontaneous activities. Invent new ways of teaching the material rather than sticking to the textbook or curriculum too rigidly. Give them real choices in how they pursue the learning objective.

❏ Making long-term commitments can be difficult for these students, so be prepared to renegotiate classroom rules on a fairly regular basis.

❏ Given Perceivers' innovative nature, sitting still through a lecture is not likely to be one of their strengths. Use a variety of teaching methodologies to keep their attention. Their energy for learning comes in bursts; it surges and slacks.

❏ Field trips that provide different, stimulating environments will work well.

❏ Have some test questions that require creative thinking and that give credit for new and unusual approaches to solving problems.

❏ Perceivers do best when there is an immediate reward for their efforts. They want to make their work interesting so it feels like play.

The following story, which has been circulated widely on the Internet, is by Jonathan Knowles. It is a great example of a student Perceiver reacting to conventional methods of teaching.

HOW TO USE A BAROMETER

Some time ago I received a call from a colleague, who asked if I would be the referee on the grading of an examination question. He was about to give a student a zero for his answer to a physics question, while the student claimed he should receive a perfect score and would if the system were not set up against the student.

The instructor and the student agreed to an impartial arbiter, and I was selected. I went to my colleague's office and read the examination question: "Show how it is possible to determine the height of a tall building with the aid of a barometer."

The student had answered: "Take the barometer to the top of the building, attach a long rope to it, lower it to the street, and then bring it up, measuring the length of the rope. The length of the rope is the height of the building."

I pointed out that the student really had a strong case for full credit, because he had really answered the question completely and correctly. On the other hand, if full credit were given, it could well contribute to a high grade in his physics course. A high grade is supposed to certify competence in physics, but the answer did not confirm this. I suggested that the student have another try at answering the question. I was not surprised that my colleague agreed, but I was surprised when the student did.

I gave the student six minutes to answer the question with the warning that the answer should show some knowledge of physics. At the end of five minutes, he had not written anything. I asked if he wished to give

up, but he said no. He had many answers to this problem; he was just thinking of the best one. I excused
myself for interrupting him and asked him to please go
on. In the next minute, he dashed off his answer that
read: "Take the barometer to the top of the building, and
lean over the edge of the roof. Drop the barometer, timing its fall with a stopwatch. Then, using the formula $x =$
$0.5 \times a \times t^2$, calculate the height of the building."

At this point, I asked my colleague if he would give
up. He conceded, and gave the student almost full
credit. In leaving my colleague's office, I recalled that
the student had said that he had other answers to the
problem, so I asked him what they were.

"Well," said the student, "there are many ways of
getting the height of a tall building with the aid of a
barometer. For example, you could take the barometer
out on a sunny day and measure the height of the
barometer, the length of its shadow, and the length of
the shadow of the building, and by the use of simple
proportion, determine the height of the building."

"Fine," I said, "and others?"

"Yes," said the student. "There is a very basic meas-
urement method you will like. In this method, you take
the barometer and begin to walk up the stairs. As you
climb the stairs, you mark off the length of the barometer along the wall. You then count the number of
marks, and this will give you the height of the building
in barometer units."

"A very direct method."

"Of course, if you want a more sophisticated
method, you can tie the barometer to the end of a
string, swing it as a pendulum, and determine the value
of g at the street level and at the top of the building.

From the difference between the two values of g, the height of the building, in principle, can be calculated."

"On this same tack, you could take the barometer to the top of the building, attach a long rope to it, lower it to just above the street, and then swing it as a pendulum. You could then calculate the height of the building by the period of the precession."

"Finally," he concluded, "there are many other ways of solving the problem. Probably the best," he said, "is to take the barometer to the basement and knock on the superintendent's door. When the superintendent answers, you speak to him as follows: 'Mr. Superintendent, here is a fine barometer. If you will tell me the height of the building, I will give you this barometer.'"

At this point, I asked the student if he really did not know the conventional answer to this question. He admitted that he did but said that he was fed up with high school and college instructors trying to teach him how to think.

The point of this chapter was to stimulate your interest in understanding and appreciating your students' different personalities and how these relate to their learning behaviors. Obviously, in a classroom full of students you will have all 16 types represented. By including a variety of teaching techniques, you are more likely to be successful with all of your students. This awareness of type should also help guide you in using more appropriate strategies with specific students who are having difficulty.

A wealth of material exists on this topic, and we encourage you to do further reading, starting with some of the titles listed in the following bibliography.

BIBLIOGRAPHY

Alessandra, Anthony J., and Michael J. O'Connor. *People Smarts: Bending the Golden Rule to Give Others What They Want.* San Diego, CA: Pfeiffer, 1994.

Fairhurst, Alice M., and Lisa L. Fairhurst. *Effective Teaching, Effective Learning: Making the Personality Connection in Your Classroom.* Palo Alto, CA: Davies-Black Publishing, 1995.

Hirsch, Sandra, and Jean Kummerow. *Life Types.* New York: Warner Books, 1989.

Hirsch, Sandra Krebs, and Jean M. Kummerow. *Introduction to Type in Organizational Settings.* Palo Alto, CA: Consulting Psychologists Press, 1987.

Kiersey, David, and Marilyn Bates. *Please Understand Me.* Del Mar, CA: Prometheus Nemesis Books, 1978.

Kroeger, Otto, with Janet M. Thiesen. *Type Talk.* New York: Delacorte Press, 1988.

Lawrence, Gordon D. *People Types and Tiger Stripes* (3rd edition), Gainesville, FL: Center for Applications of Psychological Type, 1993.

Myers, Isabel Briggs. *Introduction to Type.* Palo Alto, CA: Consulting Psychologist Press, 1993.

Myers, Isabel Briggs, and Mary H. McCaulley. *Manual for the Myers-Briggs Type Indicator: A Guide to the Development and Use of the MBTI.* Palo Alto, CA: Consulting Psychologists Press, 1985.

Tieger, Paul D., and Barbara Barron-Tieger. *Do What You Are: Discover the Perfect Career for You through the Secrets of Personality Type.* Boston: Little, Brown, 1995.

7 ATTENTION-GETTERS

If there is love and freedom in the hearts of the teachers themselves, they will approach each student mindful of his needs and difficulties; and then they will not be automatons, operating according to methods and formulas, but spontaneous human beings, ever alert and watchful.

Krishnamurti

In educationalese, this is known as establishing an "anticipatory set." Public speakers refer to it as a "strong opening." Starting your lesson in an intriguing way not only gets the attention of your students, but it can also be used to (1) establish rapport with them, (2) tell them what to expect, and (3) give them a reason to listen.

The next time you are preparing to teach your class, select one of the following attention-getting devices:

■ *Start with a provocative question.*
"By a show of hands, how many of you speak a second language at home?" Of course, this is even more effective when spoken in Japanese: "Minasan no naka de uchi de bokokugo igai no moo hitotsu no kotoba o hanashite iru hito ga nan'nin imasuka. Te o agete kudasai."*

---

*Our special thanks to Professor Akemi Uchima of City College of San Francisco for the translation.

■ *Ask an engaging rhetorical question.*
"Have you ever wondered why some clouds are thick and
fluffy and others are thin and long? Well, today we will
discover what makes them different."

■ *Begin with a startling statistic or fascinating fact.*
"Did you know that 33 percent of students who start college never graduate? Look around the room. That means
that every third student sitting around you will drop out
before earning his or her degree. Well, I want to prove that
statistic wrong by giving each and every one of you the
skills you need to succeed."

■ *Use a prop.*
In teaching a lesson on "Operating Instructions" as a basis
for establishing classroom rules with his students, Frank
put an unusual object such as an old meat grinder in a
large paper bag so that it was concealed from the students.
A student volunteer was asked to put his or her hand in
the bag to guess what was in it. Then they talked about
how it works.

■ *Do the unexpected.*
Sit in the middle of the class or in the back of the room.
Change the seating. Change the lighting. Play a piece of
music. Show a video. Any of these techniques are most
effective when they serve a purpose that is linked to the
subject you are teaching.

■ *Tell a joke that makes a point, or use a cartoon reproduced on
an overhead transparency.*
Humor can be an excellent attention-getter if done well. It
needs to be relevant to the rest of the lesson; otherwise it
falls flat or distracts the students from your educational
objective. Any humor that is offensive for any reason is
always inappropriate in a classroom.

▪ *Tell a story or anecdote.*

Chapter 8 is entirely devoted to the effective use of story-telling.

▪ *Create a mystery or puzzle to be solved.*

"Today's puzzle is: How many adjectives are on a page? I will read aloud this one page from the novel we are study-ing. See if you can accurately identify how many adjec-tives you hear."

"The mystery question for today is: How does a ther-mometer work? The first student to arrive at the correct answer before the end of the day wins."

▪ *Introduce your theme through a famous quotation, an apho-rism, a parable, or a fable.*

Great teachers throughout the ages have used these tech-niques to stimulate the thinking of their students. There are any number of reference guides available once you have decided on the main point of your lesson.

▪ *Do a magic trick.*

There are many books of simple magic tricks that you can use to grab students' attention. (See the Chapter 2 Bibliography.)

8 MOTIVATING THROUGH THE POWER OF THE STORY

Everybody is a story. When I was a child, people sat around kitchen tables and told their stories. We don't do that so much anymore. Sitting around the table telling stories is not just a way of passing time. It is the way the wisdom gets passed along. The stuff that helps us live a life worth remembering. Despite the awesome powers of technology many of us still do not live very well. We need to listen to each other's stories once again.

Rachel Naomi Remen, *Kitchen Table Wisdom: Stories That Heal.* York: Riverhead Books, 1996

Great teachers throughout the ages have always known the power of storytelling. Philosophers and religious leaders have frequently relied on the magic of stories and parables to convey moral and ethical messages in a memorable rather than dogmatic way.

Children's lives are enriched by stories, whether they are being comforted by their parents reading a bedtime story while snuggling in their blankets, enchanted by a favorite teacher reading aloud during circle time, or scared while listening to ghost stories around the campfire.

Everybody has a story. No matter what we do for a living, how much we have in our bank account, or what the color of our skin may be, we have a story. Each one of us has a story, whether it is visible to the eye or locked inside of us. We are encouraged to believe that our past; our circumstances, both physical and emotional; and our experiences are our story. Our mental picture of our life's story encompasses what we perceive to be true about ourselves and our possibilities.

The life we are born into is not necessarily our destiny. All of us have the power to rewrite our story, to recast the drama of our lives, and redirect the actions of the main character, ourselves. The outcomes of our lives are determined largely by our responses to each event. Do we choose to be the hero or victim in our life's drama?

There's an old folk tale about twin children who were put into separate rooms. One room was beautifully decorated with many toys and games; the other was a drab room that contained a pitchfork and a mountain of hay. Hours later, the child in the toy room complained of being bored, saying, "I'm tired of this, I want something fun to do." The child in the other room was happily forking hay, quickly and with great intensity. When asked why he was working so hard, he replied, "With this much hay, I figure there must be a pony in here somewhere!" Each child had an opportunity to choose his reality, as do all of us when we choose which stories in our lives that we decide to tell.

Good stories, like the best mentors in our lives, are *door openers*. They are unique experiences containing insights tied to emotional triggers that get our attention and stay in our memories. These stories can free us from being bound to decisions of the past and open us to understanding ourselves and the opportunities that are there before us. A really good story allows us to recognize the choices that are open to us and see new alternatives we might never have seen in any other way. It can give us permission to try a new path.

Storytelling is an ancient art. Long before we differentiated job titles like "teacher," "singer," "historian," or "preacher," we had the tribal storyteller, who was often all those jobs combined into one person. Using dramatic talents, the storyteller, or later the "troubadour," chanted, sang, intoned, or simply told the history and the myths, the accumulated wisdom of the tribe. All listened, not just the children. The adults listened because it helped them remember and comforted them in times of crisis. Some of the stories involved their own exploits, tales of battles they fought, places they visited, or difficult winters they survived. It helped their self-esteem, established or re-established their place in the tribe. We get the phrase "unsung hero" from the Norse custom of singing the hero's exploits upon return from battle. If someone did not return from the battle, or worse yet, if no one who witnessed the hero's exploits returned from that battle, then his bravery couldn't be celebrated, and perhaps he would not be allowed to enter Valhalla.

The story conveyed the group's values, history, and sense of purpose and often contained actual or idealized advice about how to cope with life's difficulties and challenges.

How did stories function in your family? Wasn't it almost precisely the same way? At Hanoch's family table, his father told the family of his day, and Hanoch's mother encouraged him to tell his story. Because he was a New York City captain of detectives, his stories were fascinating, sometimes even gory or frightening. Talking about his day seemed to be almost therapeutic to him. And when he'd look up and see his children looking at him with glowing eyes, that didn't hurt him either.

Then Hanoch's mother would tell about her day at work. She'd get very animated and dramatic in her narration. She'd

tell the jokes she heard that day. She'd share the victories and
defeats, the tales of the sales force and the constant flux of
winners and losers at the monthly sales meetings. She, too,
would look around the table to see an admiring audience.
Hanoch and his brother learned their family values from
those stories. They didn't call it storytelling, they called it dinner. But televisions had not yet taken over dinnertime then.
Families were still listening to each other. Only after dinner
did they retire to the living room where the TV set could be
found. Those dinners were an essential part of Hanoch's
upbringing and—only all these years later did he become
aware of it—an equally essential part of his preparation to be
an educator and public speaker! His mother's dramatic flour-
ishes and unconscious skill at nonverbal communication were
Hanoch's primer on public speaking, on great teaching.

His parents' use of the story to teach was often deliberate.
If Hanoch or his brother committed some infraction of the
rules or failed to meet their parents' expectations, they could
be sure they would hear an admonitory object-lesson story, a
tale in which someone "just like them" got in terrible trouble
for doing a similar thing. Hanoch's dad was not one of those
parents who always told stories romanticizing how great his
behavior was as a teen. No, he'd often tell them a story in
which he revealed major errors he made or really questionable decisions he had taken in his youth. And these gave him
the opportunity to criticize himself as a way of letting his
sons know that they, too, were making a questionable choice.
In the process, both of Hanoch's parents enriched his life;
communicated with him and with each other; and passed on
family traditions, beliefs, values, and skills. Those skills are
often not learned in school but at the family table.

Years later, Hanoch became a high school teacher. Apparently he was not too bad at teaching, and his new supervisor
called him a natural-born teacher. At first Hanoch was flat-

tered and, he admits, a bit puffed up by such feedback in the second year of his professional experience, but soon he realized that the credit was clearly owed to his parents; any storytelling talent of his had been modeled and nurtured by them his whole life. If you want to be a storyteller or use great stories in the service of your motivational lessons, go back to your origins. Seek the storyteller of your youth, and revisit him or her in person or, at the least, in memory. If you made any family movies or videos of that person, watch them again and again, and see what treasures are there to be mined. If that person is still in your life, audio- or videotape him or her *now*! Don't waste a moment! The natural storyteller whom most families have is an inestimably valuable resource of technique, great stories, and continual modeling of best practice.

THE POWER OF THE STORY

In 1993 a book was published that would eventually make publishing history. The brainchild of noted public speakers and trainers Jack Canfield and Mark Victor Hansen, *Chicken Soup for the Soul* was a collection of 101 stories selected, as the subtitle proclaims, "to open the heart and rekindle the spirit."

Canfield and Hansen had developed this concept that Americans were getting fed up with all the negativity in the news and with the constant cynicism and negative expectation that seemed to mark the 1980s. They believed that people wanted hope. Just as chicken soup is what your Mom would give you when your body wasn't feeling good, they thought that beautiful stories could be "chicken soup for the soul" and help us feel better spiritually. They set out to find stories that would deal with all of life's toughest and most important moments and events: life, death, parenting, loving and caring, and so on. They specifically sought stories that

would offer meaning. People would have real problems and
confront them, but they would somehow find sense and purpose and personal worth amid their difficulties. Toward that
end, they contacted many members of the National Speakers
Association and Toastmasters International who were their
friends, colleagues, or acquaintances. They called and wrote
to thousands of speakers as well as contacting clergy, both
famous and unknown, and great teachers, counselors, and
writers. They asked each, "Do you have a favorite story? Or a
story that you just love to tell at one of your speeches or sem-
inars or lessons? The 'killer' story—the one that absolutely
clinches the point you're trying to make? The story that
leaves the audience with tears in their eyes or convulsed with
laughter? That's the kind of story we want." They described
the project they planned, and many of their correspondents
sent in stories. Hanoch and Frank are both represented in this
first volume.

Canfield and Hansen didn't stop there. They'd already
written down all of their own favorites from their professional work. They read every book, magazine, journal, or
newsletter they could get their hands on, scouring them for
stories with a punch. Slowly, the stories began to trickle in.
Later, the flow increased. Many were excellent stories, but
Canfield and Hansen had to make sure to eliminate too
much similarity. They were concerned that some stories
might appeal only to them or to the kinds of audiences they
usually addressed and might be less useful or attractive to a
wider audience, so they set up a national reader panel of "just
plain folks" all over the United States and Canada. People of
every ethnicity, racial group, gender, age level, and socio-
economic background were added to the mix. These volunteers were asked to read every story and rate it on a one-to-
ten scale according to criteria like these:

1. The story has to be short. People are busier than ever. They want something that can be read in a short time, perhaps just before bedtime or in one visit to the john!
2. The story has to be true. People want inspiration that comes from real-life experience.
3. The story has to produce a physiological reaction in the reader: laughter, tears, goosebumps, weak knees, a sharp intake of breath followed by "Wow!" or "Aha!"
4. The story has to be positive—at least in its final meaning. Even if someone is contending with catastrophe, they've got to find some meaning or hope in the experience.
5. The story has to stand on its own without a moral all neatly stated at the end. We trust our readers to get the point. We don't want preachy stories, just uplifting ones.

When the book was done, it was submitted to a long series of publishers (more than 38), all of whom turned the book down almost immediately. "Not tough enough. Who'd want to read such positive stuff? We've got to swim with the sharks nowadays." Finally, a publisher in South Florida, Health Communications, Inc., agreed to publish the book. The advertising budget was small, but Hansen and Canfield were totally committed to getting the word out about this book. They spent nearly a full year doing almost nothing but promoting the book in every way they could imagine. They asked for help from a startling array of talented people—help in brainstorming marketing methods and help in getting people to read their book.

Little by little, the word did get out. Word of mouth takes time but, when it does build, it is a potent force indeed. The book hit *The New York Times* best-seller list and stayed there for over 140 weeks, sometimes number one, sometimes down to number four. It sold well over 1 million copies in its first year, 1993. As of this writing, in 2000, it has sold over *16 million copies!* The first book had a page at the back called "More Chicken Soup," which explained how readers could send in their own stories. Readers responded in droves and torrents. Now the authors are receiving between 50 and 200 stories every day at the "Chicken Soup" offices. So they produced another volume, *A 2nd Helping of Chicken Soup for the Soul*, which immediately hit the best-seller lists. The following year, the next volume, *A 3rd Serving of Chicken Soup for the Soul*, was released, and it, too, jumped onto the best-seller charts.

Hanoch and his wife, Meladee were invited to coauthor the next book in the series. They spent 13 months reading over 4200 stories, carefully choosing the best ones and then sending copies of them to over 300 readers around the country. They had selected stories from the mounds that had been sent them by mail and by e-mail and that were handed to them by readers and friends. They haunted libraries; they searched the Internet; they contacted storytelling associations and well-known writers. They wrote to famous people, and they read lots of newspaper columns and feature stories, combing, searching, winnowing, and finding many wonderful new stories. They wrote many stories themselves, gleaned from their life experiences or told to them by acquaintances. All of these went to that reader panel until they had narrowed them down to the 101 absolutely best stories they could find. That volume, *A 4th Course of Chicken Soup for the Soul*, was released in April 1997 and has sold over *1.5 million copies* to date.

At the same time, Jack and Mark Victor were inviting other coauthors to produce spin-off books such as *Chicken Soup for the Woman's Soul, Chicken Soup for the Teenage Soul,* and *Chicken Soup for the Soul at Work.* These, too, became runaway best-sellers in their own right. In fact, the whole series has sold in excess of *30 million copies*. Hanoch and Meladee are just finishing work on *Chicken Soup for the Grandparent's Soul*, and Frank is working on *Chicken Soup for the Soul of Tolerance*. We share this story with you not to brag about our own personal success or our friends but to illustrate to you the incredible power and attraction of stories, well-chosen and affecting stories. There seems to be a nearly insatiable appetite for such stories, and our mail reflects it. We are getting a deluge of mail from readers from all over the world: Kuala Lumpur, Manila, Prague, Warsaw, Seoul, Hong Kong, Jakarta, Jerusalem, as well as all over the United States, Canada, and South America. Many thousands of these letters are from students who felt touched and inspired by the stories. And thousands of letters are from teachers who have found these books invaluable for interesting and motivating their students.

Our readers tell us how the stories help them. Many write about the solace such stories provide in moments of life crisis, such as a death in the family or a major illness. Others tell us that they use the stories in their work or in their family lives. Parents tell us they turn off the TV set and read a story or two for an hour each evening. And that reminds them to tell some of their own family stories that they had forgotten to tell in the rush of work and cooking and then dropping gratefully in front of the television. Coaches tell us they use the stories to motivate the team during half-time. Clergy tell us, in large numbers, that these stories have enlivened many a sermon or wedding ceremony and, of course, provided just the right touch at a funeral eulogy. Sales managers write us about how effective it is to use such stories at the sales meeting. In fact, there have been several featured stories in publications like *The Wall Street Journal* and *The Christian Science Monitor* about the spontaneous formation of "Chicken Soup for the Soul" groups at Fortune 500 companies, where employees bring a book and a brown-bag lunch one day a week and share stories with colleagues, and their teamwork improves perceptibly.

Students write us about their teachers reading one story to start the day and how it helps their attitude about school. Guidance counselors have been using the stories to help groups of students cohere and build trust in each other. Hanoch and his wife, Meladee, are currently preparing a *Teacher's Guide to the Chicken Soup for the Soul* series.

HOW A STORY WORKS

A story can take a good lesson and elevate it to a memorable experience. In order to motivate, the teacher must connect with more than the minds of the students; he or she has to connect with their hearts, with their core values, and with their most significant experiences and memories. To do this, the teacher must first penetrate beyond the natural reserve, skepticism, defensiveness, or distance that may exist in the classroom. Some teachers begin their lesson with a personal story, such as a story about their family or a story about their previous history with students or teaching this subject matter.

Another approach is to begin with a story that is on the main theme of the lesson you are about to teach. The story need not be very long, nor need it be serious. It can be humorous or tender, serious or light-hearted, but it should definitely be personal, homey, and authentic. As you tell this story, watch the class. If the story is well chosen, you'll actually see them relax. "Ah, a story, I can relate to that. I can understand that. This class won't be one of those boring ones, and it won't be filled with useless information that puts me to sleep. The person in front of the room seems real to me." By starting with a good story, you've reassured your students that you are approachable, a real person, and we learn best from people like ourselves.

We've seen excellent teachers begin with a humorous self-deprecating story, one chosen to deliberately reduce the "us-against-them" attitude that exists between many teachers and students. By puncturing that balloon, they make it much easier for the students to see themselves as connected to the ideas that are being presented.

Stories work by connecting ideas with feelings. If you simply mention important concepts to your class, they may recognize their importance, but few will remember these points because they seem to the student to be intellectual, cold, and distant. You've offered them no personal reason to remember these ideas. Wrap those same ideas in an affecting story, and no one will forget the story or the ideas associated with them. The story anchors the concepts. Give me an idea, a fact, or a concept while you have me laughing or while you've brought a tear to my eyes, and I will never lose your lesson.

Hanoch was presenting a keynote address to a group of 1500 teachers in Los Angeles. The talk was entitled "You Make THE Difference!" and the goal was to remind them of the unique and awesome power that a really good, truly committed teacher can make in the lives of children. There were a number of key concepts leading to the penultimate one: "The time for commitment is right now; you have to behave every day as though this were your last best opportunity to make the difference in your job." At that moment he told this true story from his own life.

I was a single parent with full custody of my two little children. Living in Cleveland, I had to fly to Detroit where I was to present a workshop on stress management. The children's nanny was to arrive early that frozen February morning as I was ready to leave for the

airport. It was early in my single parenthood, and I
had a considerable amount of stress myself in juggling
my professorial job, my consulting, my housekeeping,
and my parenting. Racing that morning to get ready
and to get the children up and dressed and fed, I was
overwhelmed with the weight of my responsibilities.
Suddenly, I noticed how totally messy my children's
room was, and I just lost it. As they say, I went ballis-
tic. I ranted and raved and shouted: "How many times
have I told you . . . " and more preaching. By the time
I was ready to leave the house, I had reduced both little children to tears. "Now, kiss Daddy good-bye," I
ordered, my guilt warring with my anger. And then I
left for the airport. I drove through gray skies and
slushy, icy streets, arrived at the airport, parked, and
checked in for the flight.

The plane was an old one, a DC-9, and we strapped
ourselves in and took off into an ice storm. As we
reached 11,000 feet, the plane leveled off, and the
flight attendant began serving soft drinks from a tray
she carried down the aisle. Suddenly there was a loud
bang, and a hatch (which we could not see) blew off
the plane! All the air in the plane whooshed down the
fuselage toward that hatch. The flight attendant, startled, threw her tray of Cokes up in the air, and it
drenched some of us. She screamed. Then she ran
down the aisle toward the cockpit door, which was
jammed and bent from the force of the air column
that had rushed out of the pressurized plane.

The oxygen masks fell down from their little
hatches above us. Very few people had the presence of
mind to put them on. A 70-year-old man, sitting one
row behind me, had just recovered from triple-bypass
heart surgery at the Cleveland Clinic. He was an immi-

grant from Eastern Europe, and we had talked while waiting in the line to board the plane. He began shouting in a thick accent, "For dis God saved me? For dis God saved me?"

The plane shuddered and began a twisting, shaking, rapid descent down toward frozen Lake Erie below us. I looked out the window and realized that I was about to die. At that moment, I did not have my entire life flash before me. Instead only one image came to mind: the picture of my two little ones, standing tearfully facing me, as I yelled at them for their messy room. I realized that my children would forever carry only one last memory of their father, a mental picture of me red-faced and screaming.

I began to pray, "Dear Lord, if I survive this, if you save us from this crash, I swear I will never again leave the house this way. I will never leave my children without telling them I love them again." I am sure that most of the other people on that plane were praying, too. Whether it was the power of our prayers or something else, suddenly the plane leveled off and turned back toward Cleveland. We landed safely, and a spontaneous and protracted cheer arose from all of the passengers. Most of us hugged the pilot and copilot as we exited.

And then, paradoxical as it may seem, we all boarded an identical plane and flew to Detroit! When I returned the next evening, I resolved to keep my promise. Every time I left the house after that, I would call my children to me and say, "I want you to know that I love you. I have always loved you. I know that sometimes you may do something that I don't like, or I may be angry at you, but even then I love you. I will always love you." And I would kiss and hug them both. They were charmed by this, our newest family custom. I did it for years.

After a while, when the children had entered adolescence, they would get bored with the ritual and roll their eyes and sigh when I did it. They would even mimic me in a sarcastic tone, "I know you really love us and . . ." But I was determined to keep that commitment. One day, in a great hurry, I forgot to do the little speech and the hugs. Halfway to the airport, my cellphone rang. It was my daughter, Shayna. "Dad, you forgot to say it and hug us." Enough said, she hung up. I turned my car around and drove home. Using the cellphone, I called my travel agent and arranged for a later flight. And there were both children, standing by the door looking a bit sheepish to admit that they really loved our ceremony. We cried a bit as we hugged each other. I think that was one of my best days on this planet.

At the end of that story, the audience was teary-eyed. Tissues were everywhere, dabbing at eyes, and sniffling was heard in the room. Hanoch clinched his point. "You see, no one knows for how long God has wound his or her clock. We always think we're going to have another day, another week, another year. But who knows? Shall I teach conventionally, conservatively, holding myself back, keeping my fullest commitment in reserve for emergencies? Shall I? No! This is *it!* This is our chance to teach our best lesson, to reach out to that unreachable child just one more time. You make *the* difference! And, in fact, *only you* can make the difference!" He stopped, silent. The audience looked stunned and then erupted with the biggest standing ovation he had up to then ever received.

That is the power of a story to take your ideas and impress them upon someone's heart. That speech was given over seven years ago. Hanoch has received more mail and for a longer period of time from members of that audience than from any other group. People not only got the message, they went back to their schools and shared it with others. Many people were told that story by people who were in that room. One told her minister, and he used it in a sermon and then wrote to Hanoch. Another woman wrote him that he must have been sent to her from "on high" because she had been so burnt out as a teacher and was no longer "alive to the kids," as she put it. That speech, but most importantly, that story, offered her the path back to rediscovering her own energy and spirit in her job. That's the power of the story as a door-opener.

IDEAS AND FEELINGS

America was formed in the 18th century, the Age of Reason. We have a long-standing bias toward thinking that every problem can be solved with enough effort, thought, energy, time, or money. If I want to convince someone of something, I should therefore marshal good logical reasons, proofs, and scientific information, and inundate them with it. In actual practice, such a strategy only works for some students (Thinkers) and can alienate others, leaving them cold, unmoved, and unconvinced, or even putting them to sleep.

Are we motivated by logic or by our feelings and needs? Try this experiment: Find out the actual odds of winning your state's lottery, the grand prize. One phone call to the lottery commission will usually produce this information. The odds are astronomically against your actually winning. Ask a mathematician to explain whether or not you affect your odds by purchasing 10, 20, or even 100 tickets. The answer may surprise you. Now, the next time you speak to your class, give them that information, and ask them if it will affect their decision to buy or not buy a lottery ticket. Now, do a little more research—the Internet is great for this—and find some of the follow-up studies done on former lottery winners, how many had heart attacks or strokes, how many had marital problems apparently brought on by or exacerbated by being a big winner. Read some of the interviews with big winners about the changes in their lives—the long-lost relatives who suddenly surfaced wanting a share; the fear of their children being kidnapped; the fact that their liability increases because of their so-called deep pockets, causing them to have to radically increase all their insurance policy limits; their need for unlisted phone numbers; and so on. Now give that information to your students, and ask them if it would prevent them from buying a ticket or wanting to win. The answer? Hanoch has conducted this experiment many times. It's always the same: No one changes. They all want to win. Those who buy tickets will keep on buying tickets. "Oh, that's what happened to *them*. It wouldn't happen to *me!* I could handle it. Anyway, it's fun to dream, isn't it?"

Logic disappears when emotions are high, when need is great. The unique power of the story is that it taps in to that pool of emotion that lies just beneath the cool facade of rationality that many people affect. We must use logic, and we must offer ideas, facts, studies, proofs, and all that, but they will not work to motivate students without adding the appropriate emotional core that comes with an appropriate story.

HOW TO FIND YOUR STORIES

Most of the best stories you will ever find to use in your motivational lessons will come from your own life experience.

Having said that, we are aware of how tempting it is to see one's own life as prosaic, dull, and having few dramatic stories that might interest anyone. It is precisely because most of one's own stories come from an ordinary life that students will be able to relate to them.

Look at Your Life

Here are some possible places to find your own personal stories. Think about the first job you ever had. Anything interesting happen then? Anything embarrassing? Did you learn anything that you've used ever since?

Think of other firsts in your life: perhaps your first day at school, your first date, or your first car, if you ever got a traffic ticket or were ever fired from a job, and so on. Firsts have a way of being dramatic, at least in our memories. Intense experiences can also be the source of important things we've learned and can share.

Are you a parent? If you were telling us about one of your children, what stories about that child would you tell? Would some be funny? Would others bring a tear to our eyes?

There are life-cycle changes that stir deep emotions and are the source of much potential insight in our lives: marriage, births, the death of a loved one. Each of these areas is likely to have more than one useful story from your own experience.

In Creative Writing 101, the teacher tells us that a good story should have "tension, then resolution." The main character ought to change, learn, or grow, or tragically fail to learn or grow from an experience. The tension can come from the character's struggles, striving, or stress. Apply those same rules to your search for personal stories: When you were struggling to learn something, to get a job, to find love, and so on, what occurred, and how did it change you? What new insights or perceptions did you acquire and what caused them?

Sigmund Freud wrote about "the amnesia of childhood," saying that we all have very selective memories about our youth. To find more personal stories, ask your parents, your aunts and uncles, siblings, and friends who knew you then. You'll be surprised at what you'll learn about yourself. Many great stories can be found this way. There's an old saying attributed to Confucius: "Man was born with two ears and one mouth; it must be a message from God." By consciously reminding yourself to be a listener, you will enable yourself to find the best stories.

Take Notes All the Time

Don't trust your memory. Carry a small notebook, a pack of 3 x 5 index cards, or something on which to take notes. Make it your habit never to be without it. Those little stories you are told by your students, their parents, your colleagues, are golden. And the genius, the special spirit of the story, is in the details you may forget overnight. We have found stories to be so powerful and evocative that we even keep little notepads handy so that whenever we have an idea or an insight or are reminded of a story we can jot it down.

Hanoch was invited to do a series of training sessions in a suburban school district in the Southwest. They invited him to come a day earlier and attend their retreat up in the mountains, and he accepted. It would be a unique chance to see the beautiful scenery and experience this part of the Southwest and a great opportunity to meet the people with whom he would be working. This group really knew how to chow down! They had a good old-fashioned barbecue out under the pine trees at the edge of a mountain meadow. Rough-hewn log picnic tables surrounded the cook fire, and they were to

stay in cabins that looked like old shacks. It was really rough-
ing it, Western style. There was a lot of good-natured banter-
ing and lots of cold beer and sizzling steaks. People loosened
up and spoke with Hanoch about how much they loved living and working in that area. And then, a bit sheepishly,
most would say something about how they loved working
with their colleagues in this school district. Many approached
him to tell stories validating someone else's kindness to others or their going far out of their way to help some colleague
who was ill or struggling.

The next morning, Hanoch made his way around the
group, visiting from table to table at breakfast, asking permission to use some of the stories he had been told. He had prepared a very good opening for his seminar, but now, with
their help, he believed he had a great one.

USING THE STORY

There are three places to use a story in a motivational lesson.
The first is at the very beginning, to create a relationship
between you and the students. Your first few minutes build
that credibility as the class members size you up, evaluate
your style, and decide where to place you in their value system. Somewhere in the first five minutes, tell that personal
story, that humble incident or insight, that will establish you
as a real person in their eyes. The story also helps create a
relationship between your students and the subject matter
and you.

The second place is using the story to clinch a point, to
make a concept come alive or become concrete for the students. Statistics don't mean anything until you understand
them one person at a time. You are teaching about the Holocaust. You rattle off a litany of figures, 6 million dead, this
many death camps, that much money and property stolen,

and so on. After a while, your students' minds shut down. Bring in one Holocaust survivor, and introduce that person. Ask him or her to speak about his or her own family, losses, pain, and the class is transfixed, stunned, unable to look away. The Holocaust has become real, and Hitler's monstrousness is made plain in ways that huge mountains of facts can never do.

During the month of February, many schools celebrate Black History Month. In addition to teaching your students the significant names, dates, and historical events that comprise the Civil Rights Movement in America, tell them a story. On May 17, 1954, the landmark Supreme Court ruling *Brown v. Board of Education* brought the promise of integration to Little Rock, Arkansas. Three years later, 15-year-old Melba Pattillo Beals and eight of her friends were chosen to integrate Central High School.

As told in her autobiographical account, *Warriors Don't Cry* (New York: Pocket Books, 1994), Melba began each school day by polishing her saddle shoes and bracing herself for battle.

Arkansas Governor Orval Faubus dispatched the heavily armed National Guard to subvert federal law and bar the African American students from entering the school. President Dwight D. Eisenhower responded by sending in soldiers of the 101st Airborne Division. Nothing—not even federal troops—could prevent the segregationists from waging their campaign of terrorism that included insults and assaults at school, restroom fireball attacks, acid spray, lighted dynamite, vigilante stalkers, rogue police, and lynch mobs.

Melba survived with the help of her English-teacher mother and her gun-toting, Bible-and-Shakespeare-loving grandmother. "Dignity," said her grandmother, "is a state of mind, just like freedom. These are both precious gifts from God that no one can take away unless you allow them to."

More than one short story can be told in the body of your lesson. In fact, you can illustrate and enhance each major point you make using a short dramatic story. The danger is to use too many, too long. Your impact will be blunted if you overdo storytelling. Pick them for maximum impact, and try, if possible, to have them congruent in tone and theme, because that will help glue your talk together into one comprehensible whole. Perhaps end each story with a repeating phrase: "Another Hillcrest School success!" or "Did he give up? Never!" The rolling rhythm of that phrase punctuating the end of each story will help tie them all together.

The final use of a story is in ending your lesson. It is where you use your most powerful story, the story that you have that will absolutely touch every heart. It's the story that sums up the whole lesson because it speaks to the major theme underlying your words. Suddenly it all comes together. The story integrates the many elements of your lesson. Here is where you pull out all the stops. The students will not mind if you are corny, sentimental, or even the dreaded "touchy-feely," if your story is well chosen and delivered with your own passion clearly showing.

This is not the time to hold back. This is not the moment for you to be laid back, cool, professional, uninvolved, objective. You are finally at the moment when you want to let it all out and give of yourself unashamedly. Your students really want you to do this. Most of them would be too embarrassed to say the things you're going to say. Most really want to get something out of going to school. They want to be motivated, they want to be able to say, "Gosh, I really love this class! I love this subject! I look forward to coming here, and I love working with my classmates." However, at this point in time, there's been too much cynicism, sarcasm, and negativity for them to be able to say these things out loud. It would be uncool to say them. It wouldn't be uncool for you to say them, though, and by doing so, you allow them to agree with you. If the students were able to articulate it, they'd beg you to be fully engaged at this moment. In some African American churches, where call-and-response is the style, you hear it out loud. The speaker, whether preacher or not, says something impassioned, and many call out, "Amen! Tell it like it is! Glory!" This is not a moment for theory or for intellectualization, it is the moment for passionate commitment. Shout your story—or parts of it. At the least, vary your volume—use your voice dynamics to sustain interest. Sing your story if you can. Move your story, because you are moving dynamically as you tell it and because you are moved by it, and the students will gratefully be close behind.

Again, storytelling can have enormous power to concretize learning, to take abstract concepts or dry facts and make them come alive and vivid in the eyes, hearts, imagination, and memory of your students. It is important to use them judiciously, carefully choosing the moments where they will be most effective: as you introduce a new topic or major theme, as you begin a new unit or a new marking period, as you begin or end a school year or semester.

BENEFITS VERSUS COSTS

> Half of knowing what you want is knowing
> what you have to give up to get it.
>
> Sidney Howard

It is important to be able to articulate for your students what the purpose is of having them study the material included in the curriculum. If there is no clear purpose for learning something, then there is little motivation for investing time and energy into the process.

The secret to all human motivation can be summarized in the following formula:

$$\text{Value (Reason to act)} = \frac{\text{Benefits}}{\text{Cost}}$$

When faced with a decision whether to act or not, each of us goes through what's called a cost/benefits analysis. Whether consciously or unconsciously, we determine if the potential payoff is worth more than the likely investment. If so, we feel motivated to do it. If the costs are too great, making it not worth it, we are less likely to act.

Consider your own buying behavior. How much more are you willing to spend on a brand name over a generic product? How much is convenience worth to you; would you pay a little extra to buy an item at the corner store or would you rather drive a few extra blocks for the savings you can get at the large super store?

If you were thinking about going back to school, what would you list as the benefits of an advanced degree: stimulating professional growth opportunity, salary increase, enhanced status? What would go on the cost side of the equation: tuition, investment of time, added stress? What, for you, would be the deal breaker? What would motivate you to go or not go?

Now, put yourself in the place of your students. What are the benefits to them of doing well in your class: praise from you, feeling of accomplishment, lessons learned now as building blocks for future success, one less thing for their parents to hassle them about?

What would they view as costs: loss of status with peers, less time to spend with friends or playing video games, fear of discovering they are not smart enough or good enough?

Your challenge becomes structuring the classroom culture and learning process so that the benefits outweigh the cost as tabulated by your students' set of values. The following guidelines are offered in support of your creating a motivating environment for your students.

■ *Make the benefits explicit.*

State clearly, *from the students' perspective*, what the purpose of the lesson is and what is to be gained.

■ *Make some of the benefits immediate.*

Provide opportunities for students to experience accomplishment, success, and satisfaction right away. Typically, delayed gratification works best with more mature students. So, to tell third graders that learning multiplication tables will help them get a better job is not likely to be highly motivating.

■ *Make the benefits inherent in the participation of the activity.* Be creative in designing learning activities that are interesting and engaging. The joy of learning should be an end in itself and not only a means to some future end.

■ *Make the benefits intrinsic.*

Use your knowledge of your students' likes, talents, and goals to construct lessons that have high interest value. Avoid creating an over-dependency on external rewards, and resist the temptation to use threats of punishment.

Most young children love to play dress-up. One of my all-time favorite moments was watching my friend, Esther Wright, teach language arts to a group of hearing-impaired first graders. Materials included a full-length mirror and a large box of old clothes easily obtainable at any Goodwill or second-hand store. The children would pick an item out of the box—large feathered hat, old fur stole, high-heeled shoes, and the like. Before they could put the item on, they would learn how to sign the word for the article of clothing in American Sign Language (ASL). The children were learning their vocabulary while having a great time prancing around in front of the mirror all dolled-up in their fancy clothes. This was an excellent example of taking subject matter that could have been taught in a very academic way and bringing it to life.

If you use grades, explain the criteria for how each grade is earned. Think in terms of cost and benefit. For example: "In order to get a 'B' on this assignment, you will need to spend about 20 minutes per night for three nights studying your vocabulary words so that you can spell eight out of ten correctly. To get an 'A' will require an extra 10 to 15 minutes per night. You can decide what it is worth to you."

When doing a large project, a major assignment, or a term paper, provide a goodly number of successful papers from previous students showing how others responded to the assignment *and* how you graded and commented on their papers. This allows the students to learn your value system, to understand exactly what you are looking for in their work.

■ *Reduce the cost of learning by making it safe to risk mistakes.* Praise students in public. Offer correction in private. Never humiliate students in front of their peers.

10 PERSUASIVE PRESENTATION TOOLS

Keep away from people who try to belittle your ambitions.
Small people always do that, but the really great make you
feel that you, too, can become great.

Mark Twain

PASSION

Advertising pioneer Bruce Barton studied history's great
leaders and concluded that they had one thing in common—
the power of persuasion in their ability to talk fluently and
convincingly.

Let's try an experiment.

Make a list of the people you consider to have made a significant, positive difference in the world. People who were
able to motivate others to act, to feel, to believe. They could
be alive or dead; famous or not; historical, political, religious,
or business leaders—anyone who has inspired, moved, or persuaded you.

Next, make a list of the characteristics or traits of each
person that you feel make him or her effective and capable of
influencing others.

Note any traits all or most of the people on your list have in common.

Now, make a separate list of your favorite teachers. Include any teachers whom you remember as having been particularly good in motivating you to learn. Once again, consider what you liked about them. What made them special? Compare their strengths and talents with your list of great leaders, looking for similarities.

We would be surprised if passion doesn't show up frequently on your lists.

INTENTIONALITY

No one can be successful as a motivational teacher without achieving *intentionality.* It's a combination of factors that, when mixed together in the right container, will lead to that most wonderful and rare event, a classroom of enthusiastic learners. *Intentionality is the teacher's total commitment to and belief in education's importance, value, interest, usefulness, and effectiveness.* A teacher who has intentionality has the intention to succeed, confidence in his or her message and its worth, and the conviction that he or she can get that message across to each and every member of the class.

The students read intentionality as they watch and listen from the very beginning of your preparation or the parts of it they see and hear. How can you motivate someone else if you are not motivated? How can you encourage others to believe in something if you do not believe in it? People can be fooled by very good actors, but, as Abe Lincoln said, "You can fool all of the people some of the time and some of the people all of the time . . . " Eventually, the students do read you, and they do so by reading verbal, vocal, and nonverbal channels. Both consciously ("I really like what he's saying," or, "She's got such a sincere tone of voice") and unconsciously ("I don't know what it is, but there's something I don't trust about that guy. He seems like he's just putting it on. It doesn't all hang together"), the students sum up all the information and come to a conclusion of belief in you and your message—or not. When they do buy in to you and your message, it is because you have demonstrated intentionality.

Your intention is to motivate and to do so in a way respectful of your students. Your intention is to advocate a position, an attitude, or a new idea. Your intention is to "sell" your students on the importance and value of the material you are teaching. It is your belief and your being convinced that will convince others. Do *you* believe in this lesson? Do *you* believe in this subject?

When you find yourself eager to get up and teach, you have intentionality. When you discover in yourself a delight or even a joy in teaching on that topic, you have intentionality. When you allow yourself to let go all stops and put yourself fully into the moment, dive into the lesson, letting go of worrying about how you look or what others may think, at that moment you are the living embodiment of intentionality, and you cannot fail to motivate these students.

Now, go out there and *give 'em heaven! Knock 'em alive!*

TEACHING IS A PERFORMING ART!

It's not only the words. No lesson can be thought of as simply the words written or the words delivered to the students, although the words are very important. Word choice is not a random event—each word conveys its denotative or dictionary meaning and its connotative or associative meaning. And the context of the words as they fit together creates another meaning that may be conveyed to the students. If you get up and simply read your instructor notes, no matter how well crafted they may be, your teaching cannot be as effectively motivating as you want it to be without paying attention to the delivery process: *how* you present it.

It ain't watcha do, it's the way thatcha do it! This was the title of a Jimmy Lunceford song of the 1930s. The words of your lesson alone do not and cannot convey your full meaning nor accomplish your deeper purpose. The words alone can convey much meaning, as they must do if you send a written document to someone. If your purpose is to inform, you can probably accomplish a great deal of your goal by just these words you've chosen. If, however, your purpose is to motivate, to turn students on, to light their fire, or to make it possible for turned-off students to believe again, you must offer those words to them in a dramatic way. As Marshall McLuhan said, "The medium is the message." Your medium is yourself, your body, hands and arms, your face and its expression, your voice, tone, breathing. You become your message. Everything about you that the students can perceive is melded together with your words. You cannot divorce them. A statement made by Mother Teresa, "We must love everyone, even the least of us," would become a totally different one if those words had been spoken by Saddam Hussein. *Who you are* is a powerful statement that colors the way your words are received. How you conduct yourself, how you dress and move, how loudly or softly you speak are elements that alter what your students glean from your talk.

VERBAL: YOUR WORD CHOICE

Words are not usually chosen by accident. Sigmund Freud, in describing what we now call a "Freudian slip," taught us that there may be a purpose or meaning of which we are not fully conscious in choosing certain things to say. You are aware of wanting to talk about the problem of being overweight, but you find yourself using words like tubby, chunky, fatso, and

flabby. Most people would find those words to be negative
and judgmental. You could have said overweight, healthy-
looking, or plump, which most people would find less negative or offensive. Did you choose the words knowingly? Even
if you did not, your listeners will conclude something about
you or your message from those choices.

Shades of Meaning

Similarly, as you prepare a motivational lesson, it is smart to
discover the words that have the most positive and negative
meaning to your students. What are their buzzwords, and are
those words appropriate to use with them? What jargon
terms ought you use, and which should you avoid? Do your
students have a history with certain words? For example,
while Hanoch was a professor at Cleveland State University in
the College of Education, the dean encouraged the faculty to
form "task forces" to solve certain problems. It was a phrase
appropriated from the Navy and conveyed a serious purpose,
an almost militarily disciplined approach to confronting a
problem and obliterating it. The use of a "task force" would
have been excellent except: (1) the problems were defined by
the dean, not by the faculty, so there wasn't very much commitment on their part to deal with them; (2) the task forces
were seen as extra committee assignments given to people
whose schedules were already overloaded; and (3), most
damning of all, the conclusions and reports by the task forces
were rarely, if ever, acted upon. The faculty ended up spend-
ing several years working on these task forces and seeing
almost nothing come of that investment of time and energy.
A few years later, a new dean arrived. When he announced
that he was going to create task forces to define their mission,
there was a collective groan. He should have checked this out
before going public with that idea. Many people immediately

lumped him together, in their minds, with that previous dean and stopped listening. The point is, make a sustained and consistent effort to learn (1) what topics are of great interest to your students; (2) what slang, jargon, or special language they use to express themselves; (3) what special events or circumstances they react to most strongly—and then choose your words with care.

Connotative versus Denotative

Words have dictionary meanings, which are the general, agreed-upon definitions that, in the absence of other information, are what we expect them to mean. But words have also acquired associational meanings as well. The history a word has becomes associated with it and colors its meaning even to the point of reversing it. Words that were safe to use in public discourse have become questionable or even dangerous: for example, many words related to gender such as chair*man*, steward*ess*, fire*man*; or referring to women as girls or gals.

It is not only important to avoid words that may offend community members' sensitivities for the sake of what has become known as political correctness, it is important because avoiding them is simply kinder and more caring. In addition, unless you are talking directly about the issue of appropriate language or about sexism and/or racism, you ought to avoid these red-flag words because they distract from your main message and mission.

Every group of students has its own dialect or jargon. If you choose to appropriate some of that jargon for use in your speech, make sure you've learned the correct ways to use those words and phrases, or they can backfire and cause a reaction, like derisive laughter, that may be inimical to the point you are making at the time. Because young people are continuously updating their jargon, especially after adults start using some of it, it is probably wise to avoid trying to be too "cool," or "awesome." What is hip one month, may be tired the next. Your showing genuine interest in understanding your students and their concerns will always be cool!

NONVERBAL: YOUR PHYSICAL WAYS OF BEING AS YOU SAY THOSE WORDS

For the purposes of our discussion, we define *verbal* as limited to the words you say, in the order in which you say them. The lesson you prepared or delivered is the verbal message. Your voice qualities, tone, timbre, pitch, resonance, voice production, breathing, sonority, and so on, we characterize as *vocal*. Finally, everything else about your speech we assign to the category of *nonverbal*.

Nonverbal communication is estimated to carry as much as 93 percent of your message to the students; the vocal channel is said to carry about 38 percent of the message; and 55 percent is carried by the nonverbal, which includes timing, movement, body posture, gesture, facial expression, and so on. *Only about 7 percent of your total message is carried by the words you chose.* Most presenters, speech teachers, performers, and other professionals are aware of these estimates and spend a considerable amount of effort in training for improvement of the nonverbal channel of communication. We believe, from our own experience, that the foregoing is a fairly accurate picture of how communication works.

If we have a beautiful lesson, filled with well-chosen words and appropriate and affecting stories, and we choose to have it delivered in a monotone by a very stiff person who avoids eye contact and seems to be reading it to the class *or* we choose to have it delivered with drama and gusto by someone who is skilled at integrating nonverbal, vocal, and verbal messages into a seamless and dynamic whole, we are sure that the students will respond better, much better, to the second version rather than the first. However, if that same excellent lesson is delivered by an inexperienced teacher whose voice occasionally quavers, whose eye contact is sporadic, whose command of nonverbal is weak or nonexistent, *but who is authentically committed to the topic and concerned about the students,* the students will respond enthusiastically to that teacher because the commitment, concern, and caring shine through. These facts create credibility for the teacher. The students relate to the teacher, identify with him or her, and want the message, too. Conversely, students have the ability to smell something wrong when they are being manipulated. The teacher who is a master of delivery but has faked the commitment and simulated the caring will eventually be found out.

Nonverbal communication is important and can have a great impact on the reception of the message, but the authenticity or credibility of the teacher is even more important.

The nonverbal aspect of communicating consists of these ten factors:

1. Posture
2. Carriage
3. Facial expression
4. Gestures
5. Distance or proximity
6. Touch
7. Movement or dynamism
8. Eye contact
9. Timing and pacing
10. Congruence

As we discuss each of these factors, you may be more or less aware of your own performance in that area. It would make a lot of sense for you to videotape yourself for two or three hours on each of several days of teaching. First, watch a few minutes of tape with the sound muted and observe your nonverbal communication carefully. Next, listen without watching—listen to your tone, articulation, timing. Refer back to this chapter as you evaluate your nonverbal style.

1. Posture

Your posture does, as your mother probably told you, reveal a lot about you. Do you slump? As you walk in front of the class, what does your posture say? Do you lean on a desk? Does your body lean forward or backward? All of these are read by your students as indicators of your interest in them and commitment to your own message.

2. Carriage

How you move and hold yourself is called *carriage*. Carry yourself with dignity and energy. Walk upright; stride rather than saunter. Some teachers actually bound up in front of the room! Teachers who walk slowly up to the front of the class often convey tiredness and lack of motivation. Avoid swaying back and forth because that conveys uncertainty as well as distracting the students from full attentiveness. Plant your feet squarely. Don't put all your weight on one foot.

3. Facial Expression

Go to a mirror, and face it. Close your eyes. Imagine yourself looking very alert, energized, open, and friendly. Make your

face reflect that set of feelings. Now open your eyes, and see if
the mirror shows what you intend. If it does, your eyebrows
will be up somewhat, your eyes will be wide open, and you'll
be smiling at least slightly. Practice your facial expression so
that you know what you look like when you are feeling the
feelings that you want to project to others. Don't pretend to
be blasé or unfeeling. Don't pretend you're playing poker.
Now is the time to be animated. In an intimate conversation,
the other person is usually close enough to see very subtle
cues in your facial expression. While speaking to a class of
students, you must have correspondingly larger expressions,
so that even those in the back row can have a sense of your
animation.

4. Gestures

Hanoch's mother told him, "Never talk with your hands." In
fact, she sometimes made him sit on his hands while he
spoke as a way of training him. He wants to go on record as
valuing most of his mother's lessons, but this one was plainly
wrong. People do talk with their hands, and teachers, to be
understood and believed, absolutely must do so!

Hanoch watched the principal of a small-town high
school speak to a teacher's meeting. All of his gestures were
held in close to his body. His elbows were held close to his
sides as his hands and forearms made odd, abortive gestures.
His words were about how the faculty had to get out there
and fight, fight, fight for community support on the coming
tax levy vote. His gestures had no fight in them. Later,
Hanoch found that the principal was, himself, being micro-
managed by the school board. He probably didn't really feel
that he had the room to fight for what he needed, and his
gestures mirrored that situation.

As the motivational teacher, you've got to get the attention and interest of the class. Your gestures have to be much larger, more expansive, and communicate your confidence, your sense of decisiveness and authority. Watch any television preacher, and you'll get a fairly good idea of the size and power of gestures appropriate for motivational teaching.

Avoid weak gestures like keeping your hands behind your back or clasped prayerfully as though you were begging for the audience to pay attention. Also avoid "fiddling" gestures like repeatedly touching your hair, tapping, or twirling your ring on your finger. Keep your hands out of your pockets. If you have difficulty thinking of what to do with your hands, put something in them, a prop like a laser pointer or a visual aid illustrating your topic.

5. Distance or Proximity

One way you are communicating nonverbally is through the distance you take or allow between yourself and your students. Sitting behind a desk, for example, takes on the authority of the desk but separates you from your students and encourages you to be static, unmoving. Sitting in a circle with your students strengthens your sense of connection with them. You have to decide which stance works best with a given group of students or within the confines of your comfort level. We find that changing your position in the room, depending upon the type of classroom activity you have planned, makes the most sense.

Standing in front of the room while doing a demonstration allows all the students to be able to see you best, and then walking around the room to give them a closer look is an effective approach. Sitting in a circle for class meetings is usually a good idea. Positioning yourself in the back of the room while students are giving oral reports in front gives you a good perspective from which to support the class in staying focused.

Changing your classroom environment in ways that are aligned with your instructional objectives creates variety that helps keep your students interested. Experiment with teaching from different corners and sides of the room. You probably have movable student seating and furniture. Tell the class to turn their seats to face you where you're now standing. You'll now be closer to some students who were hiding at the back of the room. You will gain a new perspective, and so will they!

6. Touch

Touch is a powerful vehicle for communication. A hug, a handshake, a pat on the back are all examples of touch that build relationship and closeness. There are, if you construct them, places that touch can be built into your lesson to great effect. For example, you can shake hands when your students come into the room or after they have done a good job answering a question. You can pat younger students on their head or on their back to show appreciation. Touch, when it's appropriate, can be very powerful in making everyone feel connected to you and to your message.

7. Movement or Dynamism

Movement can be an important element in bringing drama and visual interest to your lessons. Harry Wong, who is one of the most popular and effective educational speakers in America, nearly flies around the stage. He uses a wireless microphone because he cannot be tied down in one place. He is at stage left and then stage right; he's down in the audience and then back at the projector table. He makes sure that all sides of the audience feel that he is speaking directly to them. Of course, movement is only one of his tools; his animated voice, moving quickly from excited loudness to an intense whisper, grabs and keeps the audience's rapt attention.

Frank designed an exercise he uses when training teachers. In a classroom simulation activity, the students—composed of the other teachers in the course—sat at their desks with two-sided cards on them. One side was labeled "ON." The other side was labeled "OFF." The students were instructed to give feedback to the teacher by having the "ON" side facing front when they felt interested, included, and engaged. When they were turned off, they were to turn their card around to the "OFF" side.

The practicing teacher could tell at any given moment how many of the students he or she was reaching and how much energy and intentionality it took to keep the entire class motivated.

Next time you are teaching, image your students with "ON/OFF" cards on their desks, and ask yourself if you are being dynamic enough to reach every one of your students.

8. Eye Contact

Hanoch's speech teacher used to say, "Speak to the very back of the room." This is great advice if the person grading you is sitting there, but it ignores the fact that everyone in front of where you are focusing will feel left out, ignored, or devalued by you. Mentally divide up the room into sections, and then make it your business to make eye contact, in turn, with students in each section. Do it randomly so it doesn't look like you're simply sweeping your eyes across the group. Pick out individuals in each section to focus on, and then vary those individuals on your next go-around.

One strategy is to pick the most resistant-looking students in each section and deliberately include them in your eye contact. Also pick the student who's smiling or seeming the most positive and include him or her as well. The latter group is included because they give you energy. Don't keep going back to the same five students, or they will feel singled out, sometimes negatively, even though you are being positive! Keep switching your focus.

Even if you are reading parts of your lesson, continue to maintain eye contact with your students. Type your main points out in readable phrases, and number every fifth line. (Good word-processing programs usually have this as a built-in feature.) This will allow you to look down quickly and find your next phrase and then look up at the class while saying that whole phrase from memory. Then you take another quick look down, and so on.

9. Timing and Pacing

Do you seem rushed? Very often teachers have so much material to cover that they put too much information into one lesson. There's really enough there for a week-long unit, not a 55-minute class period. In an overly packed lesson, you will find yourself zooming through material toward the end. The end is when you should be doing material in a way that lets the students savor your words. At the end should come your best material, your sure-fire story whose punch line will sweep the students off of their collective feet. You don't want to rush at that moment. Think of your lesson as having from three to five major points. More than this can be tiresome and self-defeating. Put each key point—in summary—in a special section of your chalkboard, so students will be cued about what is certain to be on the next test.

Timing also refers to your delivery of punch lines. A punch line is, in a joke, the laugh line, the ending whose surprise generates the laugh. The key line in a story is also the punch line, the ending whose insight, or wisdom, or content resolves the conflict of the story. You need to build to your punch line and then pause before delivering it. Use vocal cues to alert your students to the imminence of the key line. Get louder or softer, use a gesture that will be unmistakable. There are so many ways; stop, look down, get silent for just five seconds. Then, look up at the audience, spread your arms, and deliver your line. Use any sequence of vocal and nonverbal cues that will make it impossible to miss the line. We have seen stories that were absolutely perfect and yet did not work in that lesson because the teacher threw away the punch line. It came and went so fast the students didn't notice it. In fact, many jokes have a lot of repetition in them simply to build the tension that the punch line will resolve and to make it clear when the punch line arrives, because it's the first line that is different. Experiment with timing. Build the tension, pause, and count the beats. This time, deliver the punch after four beats, the next time after three. Find what works for you.

10. Congruence

Very few single nonverbal cues are the make-or-break cues that determine the success or failure of your lesson. Instead, it is the *constellation of cues* you send that adds up to the total impression you've made. Are your nonverbal cues congruent? There was a love song in 1911 that had the title, *Your Lips Tell Me No-No, but There's Yes-Yes in Your Eyes!* If you are moving dynamically, your face is animated, your gestures are large and appropriate, your eye contact is maintained, you are sending a congruent message. Nothing is out of place, and the students get the message: You are prepared, you are confident, you are excited and interested and motivated yourself—and then they can choose to be, too.

THE VOCAL CHANNEL

As we pointed out earlier, communication experts tell us that about 38 or 40 percent of the message that gets communicated comes across on the vocal channel. This includes your tone of voice, pitch, and inflection; volume; and speed and articulation.

Tone, Pitch, and Inflection

Your vocal tone, pitch, and inflection can be monotonically flat or musically varied. If it is too varied, you will have a singsong effect that most American audiences will find annoying. If it is too unvaried, it will be experienced as boring. Audiotape yourself, listen to segments, and give yourself feedback about your vocal tone. This is an area where vocal coaching can lead to big improvements.

Volume

Volume is another area where people often get stuck at one setting. Teachers can get in the habit of shouting at their students or speaking at such a low volume that even those in front of the class can't hear very well. The important thing is to vary your volume in order to maintain student interest, to emphasize certain points, and, more often, to emphasize certain parts of your sentence. Our friend Mark Victor Hansen will begin a sentence at a moderately high volume, indicating his high interest in what he is saying; build the volume and the speed at which he is talking; and then abruptly stop, pause, and continue in a near whisper. The audience is captivated. The variety and emphasis make the end of that sentence absolutely unforgettable.

Speed and Articulation

How quickly do you speak? There have recently been interesting studies about the relationship of the speaker's perceived power and his or her speed of speaking. The speakers who were seen as younger and less politically or personally powerful were found to be the most rapid speakers, and the older or more powerful speakers were found to be the slowest, who also took long pauses between words. It turns out to be a cue that the audience both helps create and responds to. When the audience knows it will be hearing from a famous person, they seem to become ready to listen and allow the speaker much leeway about how quickly to speak. In one study, researchers taped politicians running for office and measured how long they spoke, how long the pauses were between their words and sentences, and how much of their speeches were actually played on air. Then they did the same study on politicians who had left office. The findings were interesting: The more powerful the politician was seen to be, the more likely the group would let him or her start the talk late (without leaving). The audience members were also more likely to stay until the sometimes bitter end. The excerpts from the incumbent's speech shown on the evening news were longer than those shown when that same politician had been running for office. Slower equates with power, in the American mind at least.

This discussion of the verbal, vocal, and nonverbal channels was not provided for you to *simulate* commitment to your topic. The smooth and skilled but insincere teacher will eventually be found out and dismissed as a phony. But the sincere teacher, wanting to be more effective, needs to work on improving his or her use of those channels. We recommend audio- and videotaping yourself consistently over time to help you hone your ability to communicate on all frequencies. In using taping, don't tape everything and then force yourself to listen to or watch each tape in its entirety. This can be very painful and tedious. Instead, encourage yourself to audit one small segment of perhaps ten minutes from each lesson that you do. Give up rating yourself on some internal scale, because most people have a streak of perfectionism that will cause them much pain. Instead, take the position that there's always something to learn from every lesson. Choose to work on one thing rather than on long lists of deficiencies you may find. Having worked on and improved that one thing, go on to the next, following your own schedule. Be patient with yourself.

MAKE IT
MEMORABLE

I hear and forget.
I see and remember.
I do and understand.

Confucius

Academic disengagement is the term used by university researchers to describe how college freshmen feel as a result of their experience in high schools. A record 40 percent of the more that 260,000 students who participated in the study by UCLA's Higher Education Research Institute said they were "frequently bored" in high school. "This is a reflection of an increasingly fast-paced society, made more so by computers and other media," according to Linda Sax, one of the researchers.

We are teaching the fifth and sixth TV generations—children raised on *Sesame Street*—and the second and third cable generations, influenced by MTV and VH1. Students' attention span has been trained by the seven-second focus shift where quick changes in color, movement, music, and camera angles are constant and rapidly paced. (In fact, older viewers are usually disoriented and confused by the extreme rapidity of these changes on music videos. Younger people who were literally weaned on these shows are attracted by these changes. Having spent years being trained by this, we should not wonder at students' bored responses to static teaching styles.)

You may not like to think of yourself as a performer, but you are already an actor in your life's drama and in the TV show your students are watching every day. Your only choice is how exciting and memorable your play will be. Lessons are more exciting when they have:

- Interaction and participation
- Concreteness
- Practicality
- Relevance
- Interesting repetition
- Variety
- Humor

DRESS FOR SUCCESS

How do you dress for teaching on any given day? Is your "outfit" chosen to communicate something? Do you dress "up" so that you are perceived and respected by your students, colleagues, and parents as a professional? Do you wear casual clothes so that you are comfortable and your students feel more relaxed with you? Does your wardrobe change depending on the nature of the classroom activities planned for the day—an art or cooking project being different than a parent conference, for example?

Have you ever worn a costume on Halloween? Would you consider using parts of costumes on other days if it would help to facilitate learning? When Frank's friend Nicole Dooskin was in college, she took two classes, Woody Plants and Forest Ecology, from Professor Burt Barnes. "His dedication to his subject and to his undergraduate students knew no bounds, and his teaching techniques were the stuff of legends," says Nicole.

Burt was about 70 years old but would take his class on field trips where he would be the first to jump in a swamp, nibble on some tree bark, or paint his face with red clay. He would dress up like aspen trees, make hors d'oeuvres in the shape of tree roots, and teach the students Latin name songs—anything to keep them excited. At Cleveland State University, physics Professor Jearl Walker is famous for his hands-on dramatic experiments, including lying on a bed of nails and then explaining the principles behind his not being hurt by doing so.

I'VE GOT RHYTHM

Introduce the use of music and movement in your classroom to dramatize your lessons and energize your students. Different types of music can be effective in establishing a mood, teaching poetry, reinforcing or illustrating historical periods or political and social eras, for rhythm in repetitive activities, or simply as background when students are working quietly on a project.

Some research has shown that rhythm can increase long-term retention of complex facts and skills. Try teaching using chanting, rhyming, rapping, clapping, moving, dancing, swaying, tapping, and jumping.

MULTIMEDIA

In addition to music, sound effects can add vital information to your teaching. Use a tape recorder, computer, or other recording technology to capture and import sounds, interviews, and other useful data. A VCR or video camera opens a wide range of educational possibilities. Make and play videos that explore themes in your curriculum. Conduct interviews that illuminate your lessons or bring aspects of the community into the classroom.

Once when Frank was conducting a self-esteem program for a group of high-school students, he came upon the idea of using a video-recording activity as a way to help the students integrate what they had been learning. Other teachers in the school had expressed an interest in the program, so the students were asked to produce a video that could be used to communicate what they had been doing. Without any further instructions, the group was given 30 minutes to prepare.

When the students returned—lights, camera, action!

They role-played being at a party. Each of them had a sign indicating how he or she was feeling—bored, lonely, sad, upset, and so forth—as they acted out these feelings. After much complaining and negative commentary, someone finally said, "This looks like a job for Captain Self-Esteem!" In came a hefty young man with a big "S" on his shirt to save the day.

As Captain Self-Esteem touched each of the students, they turned their signs around—"bored" changed to "having fun," "lonely" became "friendly," "sad" became "happy," and so forth—and each student proceeded to act consistently with these positive feelings. The students had gotten the point that they could turn their negative feelings and attitudes into positive ones, and that the power to do so came from having self-esteem. From this, a discussion ensued in which the students explored the mechanisms by which self-esteem affects one's mood and feelings.

A word of warning: Use media wisely. Never use a video, film, or any other media without previewing it. Be selective. Choose only segments that relate to your lesson. Don't surrender an entire period to a film or movie. Pick and use only the best parts to keep it from getting boring or irrelevant. Be

appropriate to community standards and school district poli-
cies to avoid an unnecessary controversy.

GUEST SPEAKERS

Inviting outside experts to participate on Career Day or to
give a demonstration on a topic pertinent to your curriculum
can be an excellent way to add interest to your program. You
may want to involve students in helping to identify who
ought to be invited. It is imperative to discuss with your students in advance how they are to interact with the guest
speaker and what the format will be. Ask for students to
invite the speaker, create a list of questions he or she will be
asked, conduct the session, greet the guest, and so on.

Professional associations and local service organizations
such as the VFW are potential resources for speakers. In
response to a request from a history teacher, for example,
Ralph H. George of Fountain Hills, Arizona, started the "Vet-
erans in the Classroom" program in order to give students a
more immediate sense of what war was like. One veteran
from each branch of service, and from both the European
and Pacific theaters, make up the program panel. Each vet
covers the following topics:

1. A brief personal history from enlistment to oversees
   departure.
2. Arrival overseas—where, when, major battles, etc.
3. A close-call story.
4. A funny-experience story.

The panel of vets also answers questions submitted by the
students in advance, and display memorabilia that students
can view and discuss.

Some of the warnings mentioned in the section on using media are relevant here as well. Be sure you know the content that your speaker will be covering, and give him or her guidelines as to what is age-appropriate for your class. Don't let the speaker take over the lesson; set a time limit and agree on the format beforehand.

IMMERSION

What if you constructed a lesson in which the students were totally immersed in a subject: a simulation, role play, "you can only speak math," or "you are all robots responding to a program"?

Emily Burnell Petrou, another friend of Frank's, describes the "immersion" experience she had in high-school Spanish.

I will never forget the first day of his class in my sophomore year. We all sat down ready to learn the basics (*uno, dos, tres*), and I was feeling pretty confident, having heard that Spanish was an easy language to learn. In walked Mr. Hornyak, and he breezily greeted us in Spanish. *"Buenos Dias!"* he said—yeah, I could understand that all right. It was kind of neat of him to start off in Spanish instead of English, to set the mood and all. He didn't stop there. He continued in Spanish, and it became more rapid as he went along. The faces of my fellow students, like mine, had gone from amusement to terror within a minute. Surely he was going to break out of this and speak *our* language, wasn't he? After all, this *was* our *first* year in Spanish—we didn't know anything yet! C'mon, Mr. Hornyak—nice gimmick, but please, cut us some slack! After all, you're not a real Spaniard yourself—you're a blue-eyed blond Buckeye like most of the kids in this class!

He kept going. He acted as if we weren't sitting in a small Midwestern town, but rather as if we were in the middle of a cafe in downtown Madrid, or Mexico City, or Cuba, or wherever else they spoke this quick, mumbly, rhythmic language. *Help!* An older student, a popular senior, walked by and popped her head in to say "*Hola.*" We all turned to the door to gape at this girl, who clearly had nerves of steel, and listened in awe as she and Mr. Hornyak jabbered away in Spanish like a couple of natives. When she left, Mr. Hornyak said the one thing he would say in English that whole first day. "Someday, if you're willing to work hard enough with me, you'll be speaking Spanish just like Dee Dee." None of us dared to believe it, but it may have given some of us a spark of hope. All I could think was, "Listen, buddy, I have *nothing* in common with a winner like Dee Dee. This just ain't gonna happen!" Hearing this little bit of English gave a few of us the guts to start asking Mr. Hornyak questions in our native tongue, but he looked at us in a puzzled manner as if he didn't understand us and continued speaking Spanish with fervor.

The class mercifully ended with a bell that undoubtedly made us all jump with surprise, followed by vast relief. Followed then by dread that we would have to face this same challenge the next day, and the next day—and until next June! *How* were we all going to survive? My back was soaked with sweat, and I wasn't even the type to sweat when nervous. Even chemistry, my following class (which I had been dreading all summer), seemed simple after this little heart-stopping episode!

As we wandered through the hallways, everyone agreed that Mr. Hornyak was nuts, too hard, too unswerving in his wacky ideas of teaching, but what could we do about it? After all, this was high school, and it wasn't like we had a choice. Dropping classes would have to wait until college. Besides, both of my older sisters somehow emerged from his classes unscathed a few years ago. Heck, my oldest sister had spent a few weeks the previous summer in Nicaragua, vaccinating poverty-stricken children because of this man's teaching. I had to stick it out!

So the next day we all timidly walked back into his class, with stomach aches, with our knees trembling, already counting down the minutes until the bell would ring and liberate us from this crazed zealot. There he was, cocky and confident as ever, staring us in the eyes, and still rattling away in this strange language, and, slowly but surely, even the most stubborn of us were forced to go along with it. Now *we* had to speak this language, when he would randomly point to us and pick one of us out and ask us a question, and somehow we would find the courage to answer him. And guess what? It actually worked! Within a few weeks, we were all speaking *Spanish!* I mean, *Español!* OK, we weren't all speaking with the same level of fluency, but everyone was willing to give it a shot (again, it's not like we had a choice in the matter), and we left the classroom smiling instead of shaking. In no time, I was thinking in Spanish, making prank phone calls in Spanish, translating in my head the bad pop tunes of the 70s into Spanish—this language became my obsession. But Mr. Hornyak didn't stop there. We also had to learn all about Spanish culture—the music, the art, the literature, the history. By the end of the year, I was giving an entire oral report on the painter Francisco Goya and appearing in a Spanish play with classmates. Normally I hated standing in front of a class, but I actually enjoyed it and even felt more confident speaking a language other than my own. I will admit I became, for the first time in my life, a bit of a teacher's pet—I excelled in class, and I could see how much Mr. Hornyak enjoyed seeing a student sharing his amor for all things Español.

A RICH MISCELLANY

In case we have not yet provided you with enough stimulating ideas for making your educational program memorable for your students, here are a few more:

■ Construct a lesson in which you tell your class that you have laryngitis, and because you can't speak, you need their help in teaching the class.

■ Pretend you have selective amnesia, and ask for your students' assistance in helping you remember your subject.

■ Present content matter through the use of student-made puppets.

■ Set up a mock trial in which you explore the issues in a famous novel.

■ Ask your students to imagine they have a magic wand that enables them to solve the world's problems.

■ Use the idea of a "thinking cap" to help your students feel more confident in their ability to succeed. Post pictures of different types of caps for each of the major subjects being taught. At the start of the lesson, invite your students to imagine putting on their "thinking caps for math" (or spelling or whatever). The special thinking cap taps into the part of your brain you need to excel in this subject.

■ Find ways to integrate magic tricks, juggling, and games such as charades. How about a *Jeopardy*-style quiz as a fun way to prepare for an upcoming exam?

SEVEN STRATEGIES OF STRUCTURING YOUR LESSON

Professional presenters typically use one of these strategies for structuring their talks to make it easier for their audiences to follow and remember the major points. You may want to use these as ways of organizing your lessons because they will help your students in being able to recall what they learned.

1. *Build a sandwich.*
   Start with a strong opening statement, end with a powerful closing, and put some beef in the middle.
2. *Number your main points.*
   Consider the success of "*Seven* Habits of Highly Successful People," "The *Twelve*-Step Program," and, of course, "101 Ways to Develop Student Self-Esteem and Responsibility."
3. *Present your facts in a logical order—such as chronological, alphabetical, or by colors in the spectrum.*
   Putting information in a historical timeline can help build understanding as to how things evolved or progressed in a logical fashion.
4. *Pose a problem to be solved.*
   Start the lesson with an intriguing problem, and involve the students in coming to their own solution or in better understanding the solution that was arrived at by those involved. Start a unit with a question that even you don't

know the answer to—a question of values or taste, for example, where there may be a number of acceptable possible answers.

5. *Make it visual.*

   Use a chart, graph, diagram, or other visual model to help your students picture what you are asking them to learn. Make it three-dimensional and tactile. Build a model; get the students involved.

6. *Create an extended metaphor.*

   For example, "Studying English is like a trip around the world in a time machine. Some of the words we use are of Latin origin dating back to Ancient Rome. Many of our words and phrases are Anglo Saxon, and some can be traced to the Jazz Age of Harlem in the 1920s. Did you know our word *guitar* comes from the Greek *kithara*, a stringed instrument?"

7. *Repeat a key phrase.*

   Who has not been moved by the highly memorable "I Have A Dream" speech given by Martin Luther King, Jr.? Use the phenomenon of repetition to your advantage.

META LESSONS

Beyond the academic subjects you are working to help your students master, what are the life-mastery skills you would also like to impart?

Take a few minutes to do the following exercise:

Imagine yourself as having reached the age of the chronologically gifted (previously known as old age). You are retired from teaching and have been enjoying these golden years. From this perspective, reflect back on your life, the contributions you've made, the lives you've touched, and consider your legacy. How would you like to be remembered?

Now imagine receiving a letter from one of your former students. Perhaps there is one student in particular from whom you would like to hear, one of the many students who have been in your class.

Actually write a letter to yourself as if it came from this student. What would you want this student to say? What would you want him or her to remember about you? What lasting impact would you want to have had on this person's life?

After you have written the letter, read it over, and see what it says is most important to you in working with students. What is your real purpose for being in education? Having done this exercise should have put you back in touch with what motivated you to become a teacher in the first place.

This might be a good time for you to recommit yourself to your highest ideals, and to consider what you are going to do in class tomorrow that will let your students know what really matters to you.